"I believe every Christian woman needs this book. With over four million Muslim women in America, it is time that Christian women learn to reach their Muslim sisters with the Gospel. Written in a moving and empathetic manner, *Voices Behind the Veil* is a passionate plea for Christian women not only to evangelize Muslim women, but also to understand their burdens, beliefs and lives. This book should be used as a study guide for women's groups, missions groups, and all others concerned about the half billion Muslim women in the world."

—ZOLA LEVITT
Zola Levitt Ministries
Plano, Texas

"*Voices Behind the Veil* is a powerful reminder that the most liberating message the world can hear is that 'God loves you unconditionally.' This book will help Christian women lovingly share with those women who are *trapped* behind the veil that those whom the Son has set free are free indeed."

—JANET PARSHALL
Janet Parshall Radio
National radio broadcaster

"Dr. Ergun Caner is quickly becoming known as the authority in pulling back the veil of Islam. This compilation from the hearts of Christian women reveals the love of Christ for the women of Islam. There is not a more timely or critical book in all of Christendom."

'AC BRUNSON

"Read this book with   in your heart
for the voices behind

—DR. JERRY VINES
Senior Pastor, First Baptist Church, Jacksonville Florida
Former President, Southern Baptist Convention

The World of Islam
Through the Eyes of Women

VOICES
Behind the VEIL

ERGUN MEHMET CANER

GENERAL EDITOR

Kregel
Publications

Voices Behind the Veil: The World of Islam Through the Eyes of Women

Published by Kregel Publications, a division of Kregel, Inc., P.O. Box 2607, Grand Rapids, MI 49501.

Cover design: John M. Lucas

Library of Congress Cataloging-in-Publication Data
Caner, Ergun Mehmet
Voices behind the veil: the world of Islam through the eyes of women / edited by Ergun Mehmet Caner.
    p. cm.
    1. Missions to Muslims. 2. Christian converts from Islam—Religious life. 3. Women in Islam. I. Caner, Ergun Mehmet.
BV2625.V65   2003
266'.0088'2971—dc21   2003009062

ISBN 0-8254-2402-x

Printed in the United States of America

04 05 06 07 08 / 6 5 4 3 2

To Braxton and Frances Morris
for your undying support and help,
including the use of the familial grotto
in the completion of the manuscript.
Your legacy will not only endure because of your progeny,
but also through your loving sacrifice
and unconditional love.
You are truly godly examples.

TABLE OF CONTENTS

ACKNOWLEDGMENTS

The editor would like to express gratitude to the following people, without whom this book would not be possible:

To Diana Owen, for your constant contributions to the accuracy and shape of the work. Your writing is not only tremendous, but your eye is sharp toward the godly endeavor.

To the Kregel Team, who have encouraged us at every juncture of this important work.

To Linda Carter, for your unrelenting aid. You are the hands of Aaron. . . .

To Dr. Lamar Cooper, for mentoring me through merciful love.

To Jill, for your patience with an incomplete and often difficult project: me.

FOREWORD

Before September 11, 2001—the infamous day of the terrorist attacks on United States soil—most Westerners knew little about Islam. It was as though a dark veil covered the cultural, religious, and political influence of Islam. In reality, only a small percent of the Western world has understood the powerful influence of Islamic ideology. This lack of knowledge is only one reason why *Voices Behind the Veil* is such a vital book.

No longer can Christians in the West pretend that Muslims live on the other side of the globe or that what they believe does not affect us. As the world becomes smaller, their influence becomes larger . . . and so do our opportunities for interaction.

If we want to share Christ with Muslims, we must learn more about the Muslim mind-set. The majority of us do not feel equipped to witness to followers of Islam because we have little knowledge of *what* they believe and *why*. And without this vital understanding, we will not be able to speak to their minds, much less their hearts.

However, once we begin to understand what many consider the causes for Islamic oppression of women, we can address the issue with accuracy and compassion. For example, the words of Umar, the second Caliph, have been engraved on the wall of the mosque in Kabul for years: "Prevent the woman from learning to write! Say no to their capricious ways." Why have these words not been eradicated?

Many Islamic nations enforce legal and cultural standards based on prejudice against women—prejudice reflected in fewer legal rights than the rights enjoyed by men, including in some countries the legal right for a man to beat his wife.

What justifies such oppression?

We must realize that the *Qur'an* condones the beating of wives: "As to those women on whose part ye fear disloyalty and ill conduct, admonish them, refuse to share their beds, (and last) beat them" (surah 4:34). In fact, when Muhammed was asked about this statement, he replied, "What rights does the woman have with the man.... He should feed her if he eats, clothe her when he dresses, avoid disfiguring her or beating her excessively or abandoning her except at home" (hadith 7.62.77). In contrast, the Bible tells husbands to treat wives with respect. "Husbands, in the same way be considerate as you live with your wives, and treat them with respect as the weaker partner and as heirs with you of the gracious gift of life, so that nothing will hinder your prayers" (1 Peter 3:7 NIV).

Likewise, the *Qur'an* teaches that men have greater legal rights than women: "And women shall have rights similar to the rights against them, according to what is equitable; but men have degree [of advantage] over them" (surah 2:228). Hadith 3:826 elaborates on this topic. "Isn't the witness of a woman equal to half that of a man? The woman said, 'Yes.' This is because of the deficiency of the woman's mind." Again in contrast, the Bible teaches equality between men and women: "There is neither Jew nor Greek, slave nor free, male nor female, for you are all one in Christ Jesus" (Galatians 3:28 NIV).

And finally, the *Qur'an* teaches that wives are "playthings":

"Your wives are as a tilth [a field to be plowed] for you. So approach your tilth when and how you will" (surah 2:223). "Wives are playthings, so take your pick" (*Kanz-el 'Ummal Hadith* 22.858). The Bible presents a dramatic contrast: "A wife of noble character . . . is worth far more than rubies. Her husband has full confidence in her and lacks nothing of value. She brings him good, not harm, all the days of her life" (Proverbs 31:10–12 NIV).

Recognizing our differences may seem insurmountable; however, "with God all things are possible" (Matthew 19:26b NIV). In fact, the

Lord may be putting into your path a Muslim woman who is seeking something different, yet she doesn't know what she seeks. Merely watching how you live will not let her know all she needs in order to come to Christ. We have the opportunity, through this book, to equip ourselves to speak intelligently and meaningfully to our Muslim neighbors so they might know Jesus as "the way and the truth and the life" (John 14:6a NIV).

Imagine being served the most delectable bread you have ever tasted. At first bite, you can hardly believe your taste buds. But if all you do is "see and taste," you can never prepare the bread yourself. Someone must actually share the recipe with you.

That's the essence of it: We have the recipe, and we want to share it with our Muslim friends. We *need* to share it. But if the recipe is written only in measures of cups and tablespoons, yet our friends know only the metric system, we've got to bridge the gap. We must share how they too can have the "Bread of Life."

If we want our Muslim neighbors to know that there is a better way, we need to see their world through their eyes. *Voices Behind the Veil* addresses the most pertinent issues to help us speak sensitively to the hearts of Muslim men and women.

This is a "must-read" for today's informed Christian.

—JUNE HUNT
nationally syndicated radio host,
Hope for the Heart

INTRODUCTION:
THE FEMININE VOICE OF ALLAH

Ergun Mehmet Caner

Jennifer Harrell looks, talks, and acts like virtually every other young woman in Texas. Raised in Plano, she is a typical blonde, blue-eyed Texan who grew up attending her Methodist church, going to parties, and actively serving in her youth group. A bubbly, affable young woman, Jennifer would look equally as comfortable at a sorority meeting, a yacht club outing, or a Saturday football game. There is one distinguishing difference, however—Jennifer today is a practicing and devout Muslim.

In a feature for the *Dallas Morning News*, Jennifer recounted her upbringing and spiritual journey. She was for a time a Methodist youth minister after she graduated from college. Still, she had nagging, lingering doubts about Christianity. When she was approached by a Muslim coworker, she decided to examine teachings of the *Qur'an*. She notes: "When I was a Christian, I never understood why Jesus had to die for my sins. . . . I mean, they're my sins."[1]

After being warmly welcomed at the mosque, Jennifer approached a Christian minister. She asked him a series of questions, such as "why Christians ate pork, why women didn't cover their heads in church, and why Christians dated."[2] His answers were unsatisfactory, so Jennifer became a Muslim. With the support of her father, she has practiced Islam for three years while teaching at an Episcopal school. "Islam affects every aspect of your life," she concluded. "It changed my goal from living in the moment to living with the intent of heaven."[3]

This book is written for the countless "Jennifers."

We do not only address converts to Islam. We also want to speak to and on behalf of the 500 million women who have been raised in Islam. Though events of recent years have caused the Christian community to reexamine Muslim faith and practice, we have neglected our duty to reach Muslims. Thousands of missionaries have surrendered their freedoms, comforts, and even security to share the precious gospel around the world. But the task is unrelenting and daunting, with huge fields white unto harvest and most laborers back in the barn, at ease in Zion.

This book is written by Christian women to train Christian women to reach Muslim women. As most Westerners know by now, cross-gender conversation is discouraged in the Islamic world.

Presenting apologetics and evangelism focused on Muslim women, this book is unique. Many books have appeared in print to explain Islam from one perspective or another, but few have attempted to deal with the milieu of Muslim women. Fewer books attempt to understand the women of Islam from a decidedly evangelical Christian perspective. Feminist writers decry the oppression of women in social justice and education. Secularists attempt to explain the constraints of Islamic teachings on the lives of women. But *Voices Behind the Veil* is different in that we draw back the curtain on every aspect of life for the Muslim women—as female child, wife, mother, sister, and religious adherent.

Such a work could only have been written by women. Male theologians have a decided tendency to be pedantic, laborious, and rationalistic. To reach Islamic women, one needs wisdom that is biblical, empathetic, and sympathetic. I believe we have accomplished this goal. I have had the pleasure to edit this collection of writings by twelve evangelical theologians and authors. The contributors cut across the spectrum of Christian life. They are authors, mothers, speakers, theologians, housewives, and pastors' wives. Four chapters are by missionaries, two of whom currently serve in predominately Islamic countries. One chapter is written by a convert to Christianity from Islam, and four Muslim converts to Christ speak through one article.

This book also is written in a decidedly different fashion. We have attempted to allow each contributor to "speak in her own voice," with the only editing being grammatical or textual. In each chapter, the reader will be able to sense the heartbeat of the author. Their passions, prayers, and ministries bleed on each page, to tremendous affect. A number of the authors regularly speak to thousands in conferences, conventions, and seminars. Others are housewives who feel a particular burden for reaching Muslim women. In each case, their shared viewpoint is fascinating, compelling, and often heart-wrenching.

It is my opinion that men would be incapable of writing such a book. Yet that was our specific goal:

To present a work specifically geared toward raising up a generation of Christian women capable of building bridges into the lives of Islamic women and presenting the gospel of Jesus Christ.

It is indeed a worthwhile endeavor. Such a work is necessary for a few reasons. The ethics that guide a female Muslim's life are intricate and complex. Indeed, even the Muslim community itself addresses the concerns of culture. The Transcultural Education Center (TEC) of McLean, Virginia, prints thousands of brochures entitled *Seeing Through the Veil.* As a Muslim-generated education project aimed toward the business community, it seeks to explain these variances in business protocol. In the section entitled "How to Interact with the Muslim Woman," Gihan EdGindy gives six points of instruction:

1. When engaged in conversation, maintain a generous distance.
2. Islam does not permit physical contact with the opposite sex such as through shaking of hands.
3. Keep conversation focused, short, and to the point. Intimate, suggestive, or recreational conversations are not well received.
4. Use common language and avoid inappropriate, explicit, and vulgar words or topics.
5. During the conversation, staring or looking directly at the Muslim woman's face may make her feel uncomfortable.
6. Never ask a Muslim female for a date, offer any type of liquor, or a food containing pork/lard/bacon/ham. This is also a religious mandate.[4]

If such steps must be taken to ensure a proper working environment with Muslims, imagine the steps necessary to open a dialogue about Jesus Christ as Lord and God!

Certainly Western evangelical women need to understand the lives of Muslim women, since millions of them have come near. They come to our shores, live in our neighborhoods, work in our offices, eat in our restaurants, and shop in our malls. When we were unwilling to go as His ambassadors into the uttermost parts of the world, God brought the uttermost parts of the world to us. Now the onus is on us to learn how to most effectively reach Muslim women with the mercy, grace, forgiveness, and atonement of Jesus Christ, the Lamb of God.

Whether you are using this work as a preparation for a mission trip, a women's Bible study, a conference, seminar, or in private study, it is our prayer that this book will drive you to your knees in prayer for Muslim women, and then call you to rise up and reach them.

—ERGUN MEHMET CANER

NOTES

1. Susan Hogan-Albach, "Muslim Beliefs about God and Jesus made more Sense," *Dallas Morning News*, 3 November 2001, 2G.
2. Ibid.
3. Ibid.
4. Gihan EdGindy, *Seeing Through the Veil* (Washington, D.C.: TEC, n.d.).

1

TESTIMONIES BEHIND THE VEIL

Former Muslim Women Share How They Found Christ

Rachel L. Hardy

Islamic apologists often scoff at the notion of Muslims converting to Jesus Christ. The vast majority of conversions, they note, are from Christianity to Islam. They believe that few, if any, Muslims who truly understand Islam would ever convert. Yet missionaries around the world report that Muslims are coming to Jesus Christ in record numbers, even though the consequences of conversion are often fatal. Rachel L. Hardy interviewed dozens of Christians who came from an Islamic background, and has included the stories of four in this chapter. Because this chapter is also the introduction to the topic, Hardy has enumerated the basic tenets of Islam, so as to familiarize the reader with terms and doctrines used throughout the book.

In the April 8, 2002, issue of *Time* magazine, Eyad Sarraj, a Muslim, wrote a startling article titled "Why We Blow Ourselves Up." His openness and honesty in dealing with such a gruesome yet immediate issue is commendable, especially in our culture:

This is the influence of the teaching of the [Qurʾan], the most potent and powerful book in Arabia for the past 14 centuries. In the holy book, [Allah] promised Muslims who sacrificed themselves for the sake of Islam that they would not die. They would live on in paradise. Muslims, men and women, even secularists, hold to the promise literally. Heaven is then the ultimate reward of the devout who have the courage to take the ultimate test of faith.[1]

Is the price of heaven indeed the blood of the martyrs? If Muslims believe that death in jihad [holy war] is the only absolute assurance of eternal security, how desperate is the need for Christians to reach out to Muslims with the gospel of Jesus Christ?

True, there are many Muslim sects[2] and varying interpretations of Islam's holy book, the Qur'an.[3] Views differ regarding the Islamic legal code and rules of jurisprudence found in the Sunnah, and the Hadith's collection of sayings and stories of Muhammed.[4] Most Muslims adhere to the guidelines in one or all of these books for daily living.

The question Christians must face is this: *"How do I witness to Muslims who are living under this strong system of life-pervading rules?"* The place to begin answering this question is at the foundations of the religion itself.

A BRIEF OVERVIEW

Islam was founded by Muhammed (570–632). His first wife, Khadijah, participated in the recording of Muhammed's revelations, which were compiled into what became the Qur'an. After Khadijah died, Muhammed eventually married eleven other women.

Almost as influential as the Qur'an is a collection of sayings and reminiscences of Muhammed called the Hadith. There are four collections of ahadith, but the most popular is the work by Sahih al-Bukhari. The Sunnah were written by Muhammed's friends after his death.[5]

After Muhammed died, the followers of Islam split into two factions in opposition over who should be his successor as caliph or head of Islam. The sect known as the Shi'ites looked to 'Ali, one of Muhammed's sons-in-law, whereas the Sunnis followed Abu Bakr,

Muhammed's first convert and closest friend. The majority of Muslims looked to Abu Bakr as caliph, and he was eventually chosen to lead. However, the Shiʾites remained apart, and the two sects have contended with each other ever since. Of the more than seventy sects that exist today, most fall under one of the two original branches. Usamah bin Ladin and the Taliban are part of the Wahhabi sect, under the aegis of the Sunnis. This sect fiercely follows the teachings of the *Qurʾan* and the Sunnah. Sunnis strictly obey parts of the *Hadith,* whereas the Shiʾites follow them all. Shiʾites believe they have equally valuable eyewitness accounts from familial successors of Muhammed.

The other Islamic sects differentiate themselves by subscribing to various combinations of the holy books. Each has its own heritage of leaders, prophets, and customs. Many followers of Islam today are "cultural Muslims." Although they do not constitute an actual sect, these Muslims have almost a group identity. Mostly living in the West, these Muslims only go through the motions of Islamic observance.

Regardless of sect, Islam is an inherited religion. As soon as a son or daughter is born, the father whispers the *Shahada* into his or her ear.[6] From that moment, the child is considered a Muslim. Muslims identify themselves as "born Muslim" because of family beliefs, even if the *Shahada* ritual did not take place.

ISLAMIC THEOLOGY 101

Faithful Muslims adhere to Islam's five pillars:

1. *Shahada* (confession of Allah);
2. *Salaat* (prayer five times a day);
3. *Zakat* (almsgiving);
4. *Sawm* (partaking of the monthlong fast of Ramadan each year); and
5. *Hajj* (pilgrimage to Mecca).

Strict rules guide worshipers through these pillar rituals. In order for Allah's scales, which measure the good and evil in a Muslim's life, to weigh more heavily to the good side, a Muslim must perform these pillars precisely. Salvation is based upon the balance of good and bad deeds. Muslims are haunted by the prospect of dying while the scales are tipped to the bad side and spending eternity in hell. This anxiety exerts enormous pressure on Muslims to be perfect according to the laws of the holy books.

Although some people equate Islam's Allah with Christianity's Yahweh, Christians and Muslims who have studied the two religions deny that these views of God are even remotely alike.[7] This is especially clear to those who compare the conflicting hopes of salvation. The Allah of the *Qur'an* requires good works, but the Yahweh of the Bible requires faith in Jesus Christ (John 3:16). Islam claims that God can have no son, and that Jesus Christ was only a prophet like Muhammed.

Most Muslims are familiar with the name *Jesus*. When asked if they believe in Him, they will say, "Yes, Isa [Jesus] is a prophet of Allah." However, Christians would point out that Jesus could not be just a prophet, because He claimed to be God (John 8:58). In other words, He was either who He said He was, or He was a madman. This is a stumbling block for Muslims. Recognizing Jesus as God in the flesh contradicts the *Qur'an*, but so does regarding Jesus as a madman. Because the *Qur'an* records some teachings of Jesus (revised to fit Islamic beliefs), so the *Qur'an* would fall if Jesus was anything other than a wise prophet.

Additionally, Islam holds that Muhammed was the last prophet and was given the final revelation of Allah.[8] Because Christians do not recognize Muhammed and his teachings, Muslims believe that Christians have an incomplete revelation from God. They would say that pieces of Scripture contained in the *Qur'an* are truths that were gleaned from the corrupted revelation of God found in the Christian Bible.

ANSWERING THE CALL TO EVANGELISM

In Matthew 28:18–20, Jesus gave the Great Commission just before He ascended: "All authority has been given to Me in heaven and on earth. Go therefore and make disciples of all the nations, baptizing them in the name of the Father and of the Son and of the Holy Spirit, teaching them to observe all things that I have commanded you; and lo, I am with you always, even to the end of the age" (NKJV). In response to this command, Christians down through the ages have gone to foreign nations to make disciples. Wherever Christians live, lost and dying people surround them.

Although it is impossible to have a precise count from every country in the world, statistics are available estimating the percentage of each nation's population that belongs to major religious groups. These statistics show that Western nations are increasingly saturated with Muslims. In order to be more effective vessels for the Lord's service, it is imperative that Christians become familiar with all the major religions in their area.[9]

LIFTING THE VEIL

How can we, as Christians, follow Jesus' Great Commission among the Muslims who live all around us—especially Muslim women? One way is to see how the Lord has already drawn some out of Islam into a relationship with Himself. Through the personal stories of four women, we hope to educate and encourage Christian women to share the good news about Jesus with their Muslim neighbors, friends, and acquaintances.

The women who consented to share their testimonies here have taken a dramatic step. Even allowing their first names to be published places them at risk from other Muslims. However, their faith in Christ and their love for non-Christians gives them a boldness to speak openly. Each woman's meeting with God is unique. What the Lord chooses to use in one person's life is not necessarily how He will work in another's. It is important to remember that many other Muslim women, whose stories we might have shared, have followed the call to new life in Jesus Christ.

Terra

Terra, 28, was reared as a Sunni Muslim in Denver, Colorado, and now resides in Amarillo, Texas. Her mother is a Caucasian American with a Christian heritage who married a Palestinian. Her husband would not allow her to share anything about Christianity with her children. Although Terra did not grow up in a fully practicing Muslim household, her devout aunt often took her to the mosque to pray and encouraged her to memorize the *Qur'an*. Terra participated in the fast of Ramadan and the feast of *Eid al-Fitr*, as well as other cultural activities in the Muslim community. However, Terra came to resent and question the belief system that surrounded her "all the time."

> My mother made it clear she was not a Muslim. I quickly grew enraged by the special treatment directed to my two brothers and male members of the family. We were instructed never to look any man in the eyes. It was constantly drilled into us that men were far beyond women in worth. When we were alone, I asked my mother questions about Jesus and His atoning death, but she warned me of the repercussions if I ever uttered Jesus' name. My father made it clear that any steps my mother took outside his consent would result in severe consequences by him and his family. I had that yearning to know Jesus, but the fear ran too deep.

Other women who grew up in such an environment and later became Christians report that they felt a peace in the gospel message when they first heard it. For Terra,

> That truth materialized when I was alone with the TV turned to Billy Graham at one of his crusades. Then I had the cold hard facts, if you will, that I fell desperately short of the glory of God. I believe I then received Christ as my Savior. When I prayed the sinner's prayer, unbelievable joy swept through me, and, oh, how I longed to share the Good News! But I was

ruled by fear and guilt. I was terrified of my father and for the safety of my two younger brothers and sister and mother.

Sixteen or seventeen years elapsed between Terra's first encounter with Jesus Christ and the moment when she actually accepted Him as her Lord and Savior. Having been reared in a legalistic religion, she still finds it hard to accept God's unconditional love. She knows that legalism is a trap, and that there is nothing she can do to earn God's love for her, because He has given it to her freely. She realizes that "the Allah I grew up with is, in essence, the polar opposite of the one true God." To Terra, the most enticing aspect of Christianity was His atonement and complete forgiveness of sins:

> Legalism and condemnation are pointless. The only tool is love. They [Muslims] must be loved to Jesus. Most, if not all, Christians I come across are completely ignorant of Islamic culture and practice. I find myself explaining over and over a condensed version of Islam and its history. Only through recent events—9/11—has anyone seemed remotely interested. Witnessing to Islamic women would revolutionize the world, for they are the ones who raise the sons. They can change the world. It's a large task but a worthy goal. We must know where they are coming from in terms of how they see things and the consequences of converting.

If Terra could speak to every Muslim woman at one time, without fear of consequences, she said she would love to share with each that "God loves you so much, and He is the one true God. His blessings await you. He desires for you a life of freedom and joy—and you are worth it. To Him you are as good as any man and just as worthy of His love."

As was Terra's mother, many young women are lured into Islam by Muslim men. In order to marry a Muslim man, the woman must "convert" on paper. Often believing they are discovering the whole truth for the first time, these women abandon faith backgrounds that never seemed real or important to them in order to pursue love and the close culture of Islam. Such was the case with Katrina, our next example.

Katrina

Katrina, 46, was reared in the southern United States as a nominal Christian, but she eventually came to believe that Christians were deceived. When Katrina married a Muslim man, she converted on paper, as is required, but six years later, while in Syria during the month of Ramadan, she made the decision to fully pursue Islam.

Intending to be a faithful Muslim, she prayed five times a day, covered herself completely, fasted at Ramadan, had Qur'anic studies in her home every Friday night, and brought others into Islam. But after seven years of witnessing the abusive side of Islam and having become confused and desperate, she cried out to God to reveal truth to her. That day, the prodigal returned to her heavenly Father.

Katrina states, "I could not stop crying, because I had denied Christ . . . as Peter did, . . . but the peace that passed all understanding was back." She told her husband of her decision to make Jesus her Lord and his response was swift. "My husband divorced me [in the Islamic fashion] when I refused to come back to Islam. I lost my marriage and lived in hiding off and on for a year because of fear."

Katrina has since founded Zennah Ministries and written several books.[10] When her ex-husband's family discovered her authorship, his uncle told her that he did not appreciate what she was doing, but he admired her stand. She says that Christians lack boldness with Muslims, and boldness is a quality that Muslims respect: "When you talk with a Muslim, one of the first things out of their mouths is that they are Muslim. . . . But Christians seem to try and come in the back door. Muslims view it as not being proud of Christ or [as an admission] that our beliefs are weak."

Terra and Katrina are from the United States, but other women came to Christ as newcomers to Western culture who knew little or nothing about Christianity from their background. Ultimately they came to escape the oppressive Islamic culture in which they were living.

Sharareh and Parichehr

Sharareh, 34, and Parichehr, 40, both former Shiʾite Muslims, came from Shiraz, Iran, and now attend church together in Dallas, Texas. They accepted Christ through the presentation of the gospel by the pastor of a church they had visited, but it was not an immediate decision for either.

Sharareh first heard the gospel seven years before she made the choice to accept Jesus as Lord of her life. In Iran, she questioned Islam because of its preferential treatment toward men. She also had contact with a Christian aunt and friends in her Iranian neighborhood. One month after she moved to the United States, she became a Christian.

"I asked my family why [men should have preference over women], and they told me it was because the *Quʾran* says so. I did not feel like that was a good answer. My family would not get angry, but they told me that if I asked any more questions Allah would punish me in some way."

The fear of Allah's impending punishment was always a concern for Sharareh, but she still did not feel at peace inside. Logic told her that the denial of basic human rights was not something God should sanction. She continued to search for answers. During this time, she and her husband decided to bring their children to the United States, so that they could get a better education.

Even while she struggled with visa problems in Iran, Sharareh came to believe that God would reveal Himself and would lift the problems she felt. Before leaving Iran, she made a pilgrimage to a holy place in Iran, but "I didn't feel anything when I went there and came back." When she arrived in the U.S., she visited a church where the pastor "was speaking on the topic of God taking your burdens for you, and I realized God was calling me, and I felt at peace being there."

Many Muslims are accustomed to acting on the basis of dreams. Sharareh believes that God used dreams to speak to her heart. Former

Muslims frequently say that God has spoken to them in a dream or vision, and some may have to be cautioned that such an experience is not a prerequisite for conversion or spiritual enlightenment. Islam is a religion based upon mystical experiences, and Muslims are familiar with the idea, so perhaps the Holy Spirit does speak on this subjective, emotional level to draw Muslims to the truth. Although Islam claims that Muhammed's revelations are from Allah through the angel Gabriel, experiences of peace and love are characteristic only of the true God who is recognized by Christianity.

Parichehr's testimony contains elements of violence that sometimes are portrayed by the media as characteristic of a typical Muslim woman's life. It is important to understand that these circumstances are not typical, although they do occur. Some violent Muslims exact a great price from anyone, especially a woman, who leaves Islam. However, not all Muslims or Muslim countries tolerate or condone violence.

Prior to the 1979 overthrow of the shah in Iran, women could wear Western-style clothing if they wished and even compete in the market-place. However, under the Islamic Republic in power since 1979, conservative clerics have enforced strict Islamic laws.

Parichehr wanted to obtain an education and pursue a career, so she was allowed by her parents and the government to go to the university after the revolution. At the university, however, she was caught in a violation of the new rules:

> One day my roommates and I went for an early morning walk. Although we were wearing the *Hijab*, which covers all of the head except for the face, and a *Chador*, which rests like a sheet over the body, as the dress code guidelines specify, someone saw us out and reported us to the principal saying that women shouldn't be out so early and that we were improperly dressed. I received a letter from the principal saying that if we were seen walking that early in the morning again we would have acid thrown in our faces.

The injustice and threat of physical harm, which she and her friends experienced, served only to distance her from Islam. Parichehr later had the freedom to speak openly to a sympathetic husband about her feelings. She explained that "it's not the outside [makeup or clothing] that counts; it's the heart that matters. I was not afraid to tell him. I just wanted him to see my point. When I explained my views to him he understood and accepted them. When his family saw that he was still happily married to me after ten years, they, too, accepted my wearing of makeup and my own choice of clothing."

These human rights issues caused Parichehr to question Islam's stance on the equality of men and women. The doubts she was already feeling, along with the interest she had in Christianity after watching the *Jesus* video at a Christian's house in Iran, drove her and her husband to the life-changing decision to come to the United States. They decided that life would be better for their children if they could get an American education, and Parichehr's life would be easier if she did not have to live under Islamic rules.

In the U.S., her children received the education she wanted for them, and she was finally free from the oppressive Islamic rules, but she was still miserable. She and her husband were having financial difficulties, and she was unable to make friends. Things were not working out as she had hoped.

I met Josephine in an Iranian grocery store after we moved to the U.S. She noticed I was upset and asked me what was the matter. I told her I was upset and that I wanted to go back to Iran. Josephine told me she knew of a place where I could go to get peace. I argued with myself for a month whether I should go to this Christian church or not. I felt guilty for even considering it. I finally decided to come and I saw how caring the Christians are. However, I still felt guilty because of the Islamic teaching that Allah would punish me for converting to another religion. I was scared he would punish me for going to this church. In Islam, Allah is introduced as a fear-causing, vengeful, very angry god. Your actions damn you to hell. You live in fear.

Because of the love of the Christians at her church and the peace she received when she heard the pastor's preaching, Perichehr became a Christian forty days after her first visit to the church. "All the questions I had before as a Muslim were answered in those forty days. I felt peace when I accepted Christ. A lot of worries were taken away. I no longer cared about worldly worries because I had so much peace."

Both Parichehr's and Sharareh's husbands have accepted Christ through the ministry of their pastor's preaching and gospel presentations. These two women found the peace for which they were searching in Jesus Christ.

As these stories suggest, many Muslims are searching for something to fill a personal life void that Islam cannot fill. And although it is true that coming into a right relationship with Jesus Christ produces peace and joy, it only is through the growth and cultivation of that relationship that the "God-shaped hole" remains filled, as Christ continually and completely satisfies us.

METHODS FOR MINISTRY

God works through a variety of circumstances to bring people to a saving faith in Him.[11] Through these personal encounters with Christ, we know that there are several things we *should* do when sharing Christ woman to woman. These principles can be summarized by the acronym B.E.L.T.

> *Be bold* and confident as you share your faith.
> *Educate* yourself about Islam.
> *Love* your Muslim contact as a genuine friend.
> *Tell* her you know how she can find peace.

Likewise, there are things that we should *not do* as we tell Muslims about Christ:

- Do not condemn Muslims personally.
- Do not condemn Muhammed, Allah, or Islam.

- Do not be insensitive to Islamic customs and practices.
- Do not treat Muslims as a mission project. Insincerity glares across cultural and language boundaries.

The spiritual journey of a Muslim toward Christ can take years, and there is no tried-and-true method. Some believe when they hear the gospel for the first time, but it can require years of friendship and the Lord's work through circumstances before they will listen. While our Muslim friends work through this process, we must be sensitive to the possible ramifications of a decision to become a Christian. Devout Muslims will consider converts to have deserted their faith. They may be disowned or worse. Becoming a Christian will result in many cultural changes, as well. Therefore, do not be discouraged if it appears that they are procrastinating in making a decision to accept Christ. Press on in your relationship and continue to pray earnestly for them.

The Great Commission requires us to go into the world and preach the gospel, baptize, and *train disciples to obey Christ's commands.* All too often, new Christians are left to fend for themselves spiritually, without instruction or discipleship. Spiritual mentoring is even more essential for former Muslims, who may be giving up much, including family relationships, to believe in Jesus Christ. Former Muslims have an incredible opportunity to shine light into the lives of their Muslim friends and family. Help them learn how to do that. Teach them what you know about God and the Bible.

NOTES

1. As cited in Phil Roberts, "The Victims of 9-11," *The Midwestern*, June 2002, 2.
2. Sects are the divisions of believers within Islam who are grouped by doctrine, much as Baptists, Lutherans, and Presbyterians are in Christianity.
3. To read the *Qu'ran* online, see http://www.kuran.gen.tr/html/english/.
4. For more information on the Sunnah and the *Hadith,* see http://isgkc.org/sunnah.htm.

5. For more information on the history of Islam, see http://www.fordham.edu/halsall/islam/islamsbook.html.

6. The *Shahada* is the Islamic creed: "*There is no god but Allah. Muhammed is the messenger of Allah.*"

7. Ergun Mehmet Caner and Emir Fethi Caner, *Unveiling Islam* (Grand Rapids: Kregel, 2000), 243.

8. For more information on the differences between Christianity and Islam, see http://www.gospelcom.net/faithfacts/islam.html.

9. For information on other cults, sects, and religions from a Christian perspective, see http://www.namb.net/root/resources/beliefbulletins/.

10. For more information on Zennah Ministries, see http://www.zennahministries.com or write to Zennah Ministries, Inc., P.O. Box 1235, Holmes Beach, FL 34218.

11. For more information on ministry to Muslims see http://www.answering-islam.org.

2

KHADIJAH'S CADRE

The Wives of the Prophet Muhammed

Ruqaya Naser

In recent days, Muhammed's marriages have come under scrutiny by Western scholars. Though Surah An-Nisa 4:3 is explicit that no Muslim man is to have more than four wives, Muhammed had more at some later times in his life. In this chapter, Ruqaya Naser gives a brief biography of Muhammed's mother and of each of the thirteen women he married. In her writing, Naser uses the Middle Eastern method of oral narrative, the timeless tradition of storytelling. Naser, a former Muslim herself, sheds light on these women and their effect on the Islamic community. Naser's stirring testimony of her own journey from being a devout Muslim woman to becoming a courageous believer in Christ gives her a tremendous insight on this little-studied dimension of Islamic history.

Khadra was a tall woman, yet age had invaded her body and she bent low over her cane. The years had taken over her hearing as well as her posture. I remember that when I spoke to her, she would come close to me and ask me to repeat my sentences several times before she could hear me. One of her eyes had been surgically removed because the doctor felt it would be best for her migraine headaches. Unfortunately, removing the eye did not help the headaches, so she continued to suffer. Khadra was my grandmother.

Born and raised in the Middle East, she grew up not knowing how to read or write, but Arab culture and the Islamic religion were ingrained in her heart. She knew no other country, language, religion, or culture. She married at a very young age, and she was widowed at a very young age, as well. Her brothers tried to marry her off again, but she refused to give up her five children. Instead, she opted to pay her brothers for the dowry they would have received for her second marriage and to raise her children as a single mother. With no support and a war in her country, she moved east of the Jordan River with her children. Those circumstances, she believed, drew her closer to Allah.

There are many things I didn't know about my grandmother, but I had the opportunity to get to know her during the three years I lived with her after my father decided I should go back to Jordan to learn my language and my Islamic religion. I came to know her as the grandmother who couldn't see or hear me well, but a woman who was devoted to Allah. Even though she couldn't hear me, she was able to hear the call to prayer every morning. The first words that came out of her mouth when she woke up were, "I bear witness that there is only one God, Allah, and that Muhammed is the Prophet of Allah." She spent several hours in prayer every morning and made sure she fulfilled her duty in praying five times a day. Every night before Grandmother went to sleep, she would take her prayer beads to bed and recite, "Praise be to the Almighty Allah." She dutifully performed the five pillars of Islam: confession, prayer, fasting, giving alms, and visiting Mecca. She never told me who taught her how to pray, but I know she did it constantly and consistently.

As I look back at my grandmother's devotion to Allah and her religion, I recall how she taught me to be a devout Muslim. But in 1998, my allegiance moved from Allah to Jesus. I write this chapter with mixed emotions as I think of my grandmother and wonder whether she might have come to know the true God. Was she given a chance to explore another faith besides the faith of her family? Did she really know about Muhammed, his life, his mother, his wives, and his daughters? Because of my allegiance to Jesus and my dedication to my grandmother, the woman who taught me the disciplines of spiritual life, I write.

AMINAH: MOTHER OF THE PROPHET

It would be incomplete to talk about the women in Muhammed's life without mentioning his mother, though very little is recorded about her. We know that her name was Aminah, and she was the daughter of Wahb Abdu-Munaf, son of Zorah-bin-Kulab. Aminah, the blushing bride, married a man named Abduallah and conceived a child. Before Aminah gave birth, her husband died while returning from Medina. Most Muslim scholars claim that Aminah received a glad tiding in a dream of a son she would call Muhammed. In April of 570, Aminah gave birth to the boy who would become the Prophet of Islam.

When Aminah didn't have enough milk for the baby Muhammed, she gave him to a slave girl named Thaubiyah to nurse. It was customary for a child to be suckled by a woman other than his mother, and for that reason Muhammed was sent to live with a woman named Haleemah Sadiyah. Muhammed lived with Haleemah for a few years until she sent him back to his mother.

Aminah decided to visit her husband's grave and set out for Medina with her father-in-law and the young Muhammed. After spending a month there, she became ill on her journey home, and died, leaving Muhammed to his grandfather. To add to the young child's pain, Muhammed's grandfather died a few years later, and Muhammed went to live with his uncle.

Despite these afflictions, Muhammed grew up to be a tradesman. At the age of twenty-five, he went to work for a woman named Khadijah, a decision that changed his entire life.

MOTHERS OF THE BELIEVERS

Khadijah Bint Khuwailid

Khadijah was a young woman living in the town of Mecca. Her father's name was Khuwailid and her mother's name was Fatima. She fell in love with a man named Abu Halah. After a few years, he died, leaving Khadijah with two young children, Hind and Harith.

Determined to go on, she married another man named Atique, and they had a daughter they also named Hind. But then Atique died, leaving Khadijah a widow for the second time. With three children and a business left by one of her husbands, Khadijah dedicated herself to business and hired Muhammed to work with her servant Maisarah. The men worked well together, and Khadijah was impressed with Muhammed's hard work.

She entrusted him with her wealth, and one day she realized she was ready to entrust him with her heart. Nervous and unsure, Khadijah sent her friend Nafisah to inform Muhammed of her desire to marry him. Muhammed expressed interest and went to ask for her hand. Khadijah was so excited that she accepted the offer immediately. He offered twenty camels as a dowry for Khadijah and she was so overjoyed she asked her servant to dance and beat the tambourine. Khadijah's cousin, Waraqah bin Nawfal, officiated at the wedding.

Khadijah loved Muhammed so much that she gave him a servant named Zaid and offered to him as a servant Haleemah (the woman who had suckled him), as well as camels, goats, and other goods. She also entrusted her business to him as she stayed home to care for her children. Khadijah and Muhammed were the parents of four young girls named Zainab, Ruqaya, Umm Kulthum, and Fatima.

Life was normal for Khadijah and Muhammed until one day when he began to visit Cave Hira to meditate. Muhammed was forty years old and Khadijah was fifty-five at that time. It could be that Muhammed began to meditate in order to connect with his spiritual side, or possibly he simply needed a break from the urban pace of Mecca. As he was meditating in Cave Hira, he felt the presence of a spirit. The spirit identified himself as Gabriel, an angel of God, and informed Muhammed that he was to be the final prophet. Terrified by the experience, Muhammed ran home to tell his wife everything that had happened. Khadijah took a blanket and covered her husband's shaking body. She comforted him and asked Waraqah bin Nawfal to talk to him. After a lengthy visit, Waraqah confirmed to Muhammed and Khadijah that the angel was truly from Allah and that Muhammed was called to be one of his prophets. Khadijah believed and became the first Muslim convert.

It was harder for Muhammed to convince the people of Mecca that he had been called by Allah. He and Khadijah faced opposition and hardship for ten years, as Muhammed took Allah's message to the Arabs, until Khadijah died at the age of sixty-five. Before Khadijah died, she believed that Allah promised her a place in paradise because she was committed to helping her husband with his mission.

Muhammed never had a second wife while he was married to Khadijah, but now he was a lonely fifty-year-old widower in need of a companion.

Sawdah Bint Zam'ah

After the many ups and downs in her life, Sawdah never imagined that she would be married to Muhammed. She had embraced Islam with her husband, As-Sakran, during the early years of Muhammed's calling. They were living in Mecca with their son, Abdur-Rahman, at the time Muslims were being persecuted by the rulers of Mecca. To escape this persecution, they fled to Abyssinia (modern Ethiopia). After living there for a time, the family returned to Mecca, where As-Sakran died. During a war, Abdur-Rahman died as well. Sawdah was fifty years old and without a husband or son.

While Sawdah was in Mecca, a mutual friend suggested that Muhammed and Sawdah might marry. Muhammed agreed, in part because Sawdah could look after his four daughters while he traveled. He paid a dowry of four hundred *dirhams* and they lived together as husband and wife.

Sawdah was known for her generosity while she was married to Muhammed. A story is told that when Caliph Umar sent a bag of *dirhams* to her, she immediately ordered a maidservant to distribute the money to the needy. After many years, she died in 55 A.H. (After *Hijrah*).

After Muhammed was married to Sawdah, he received a revelation from Allah, allowing him to marry as many wives as he pleased: "You

[Muhammed] may defer any of them you wish and take to yourself any you wish, and if you desire any you have set aside, no sin is chargeable to you" (surah 33:51). He began to accumulate wives.

Aishah Bint Abu Bakr

Ancient Arabia was a harsh culture in which to be a young girl. In pre-Islamic days, husbands reacted with disgust when their wives gave birth to a girl: "And when the news of the birth of a female child is brought to any of them, his face became dark, and he is filled with inward grief. He hides himself from the people because of the evil of that whereof he has been informed. Shall he keep her with dishonor or bury her in the earth" (surah 16:58–59). This surah refers to the practice of burying girls alive. Many young girls were killed before Muhammed received a revelation from Allah that forbade Arabs to kill their young daughters. The verse portrays Allah on the judgment day, asking guilty fathers why they had killed their innocent daughters. "And when the female infant buried alive shall be questioned: For what sin was she killed?" (surah 81:8–9).

One whose life was spared because of Islamic teaching was Aishah bint Abu Bakr.

Muhammed, at the age of fifty-one, received a revelation from Allah informing him that Aishah would be his wife. Although the revealed bride was only six years old at the time, her father, Abu Bakr, agreed to an immediate marriage. Abu Bakr was Muhammed's best friend and confidant. Much is written about Abu Bakr, but we know little of his relationship with his daughter, beyond this act of giving her away. Law could forbid fathers from killing their young daughters, but this doesn't mean that fathers truly loved and protected their daughters. Whether at her father's request or by Muhammed's decision, the union was not consummated until Aishah was nine (Sahih Bukahri 7.62.64).

Aishah was a bright young girl, who memorized many of Muhammed's sayings and traditions (ahadith) as well as parts of the Qur'an. She was playful as well. A tradition is recorded that

Muhammed raced his young wife and played games with Aishah and her friends.

Despite the great age difference, only one crisis is told from the marriage. When Muhammed journeyed, he decided by lots which wife to take. For one expedition the lot fell to Aishah, and all was well until the caravan's return trip. Aishah left camp to relieve herself and later discovered that she had lost her necklace. While she returned to search for it, the caravan broke camp and left. In the dark, no one noticed that Aishah was not on her camel. Scared and unsure, she wrapped herself in a blanket and waited for someone to return for her. A traveler found her all alone the next morning and escorted her back to town. The rumor spread, however, that Aishah and the man had had sexual intercourse, and Aishah's reputation was tarnished. She returned to her parents for a month until Muhammed finally came to retrieve her. She was hurt that he had taken so long and offended that he seemed unsure about whether to believe her. Then Muhammed received a revelation from Allah informing him that all the accusations against Aishah were false.

Aishah lived with her husband and a growing number of other wives for nine years until Muhammed died.

Hafsah Bint Umar Bin Khattab

Hafsah's father, Umar, was a strong Muslim leader and Muhammed's second closest friend and confidant. Naturally, Hafsah grew up following Islam herself. She married a good Muslim man named Khunais at a young age. Khunais was dedicated to Islam, and he fought in the Badr War. He died from injuries sustained in the war, earning him the right of martyrdom. Hafsah was devastated and all alone, as she did not have any children from Khunais. Concerned for his daughter, Umar asked Abu Bakr and Uthman to marry his daughter, but both men refused. Umar was thrilled when Muhammed agreed.

Hafsah was twenty-two when she married Muhammed, who then was fifty-five. She was literate, and Abu Bakr kept the written *Qur'an* with her. She was well known for her devotion to prayer and fasting. Hafsah lived to be fifty-nine years old.

Zainab Bint Khuzaimah

Zainab's nickname was Umm-ul-Masakeen, "mother of the poor and the needy," because she had a heart of compassion. Unfortunately, her heart was broken when her husband, Abdullah bin Jahsh, was martyred in the Uhud War. Muhammed felt pain for her grief and offered to marry her. Zainab lived only three more years, dying at the age of thirty-three.

Hind Bint Abi Umaya

Hind bint Abi Umaya was called Umm Salamah, "the mother of Salamah." She and her husband, Abdullah bin Abdul-Asad, were among the first to embrace Islam. During the period of persecution in Mecca, they fled twice to Abyssinia and once to Medina. On their way to Medina, the tribe of her family stopped them and told Abdullah that they would not allow him to take Hind with him. Abdullah's family demanded that he leave his son with them. Ultimately, Abdullah left for Medina without his wife or son, and Hind lost both her husband and child.

Every day for a year, Hind visited the place where her family had been broken to sit and weep. A family member took pity on her and asked the clan to allow her to go to her husband in Medina. Finally, Hind was given permission to leave, but she refused to go without her son. Abdullah's family relented and returned Salamah. With great joy, she traveled to Medina to her husband. Soon she conceived and gave birth to a daughter, Zainab.

Abdullah left his wife and children to fight in the Uhud War. He came home with a deep wound and died, leaving his wife widowed and the only parent to two children. After the time of mourning, Muhammed proposed to Hind, who was then thirty-two, but she was unsure that she should marry someone who already had several wives. "O messenger of Allah," she said, "I am a jealous woman, I am advanced in age, and I have many children."

Muhammed replied, "As for your jealousy, I will pray to Allah the

Almighty to take it from you. As for your age, I am older than you (at the time he was fifty-six). As for your many children, they belong to Allah and his messenger." Hind agreed and married Muhammed. They were married for seven years until his death.

Hind was a well-educated woman who recited many of Muhammed's traditions. She was known for her wisdom and gave judicious advice to Muhammed.

Zainab (Barra) Bint Jahsh

Her real name was Barra, but Muhammed, her paternal cousin, changed her name to Zainab after she embraced Islam. Zainab was the daughter of Abd al-Mutalib, the uncle who had taken in Muhammed after his grandfather died. When it came time for Zainab to be married, Muhammed felt she should marry Zayd, his adopted son. Zainab and her brother rejected the idea. Zayd had been Muhammed's slave before the adoption. However, Muhammed insisted that Allah had revealed that Zayd must marry Zainab. Allah even sent Qur'anic verses to affirm his desire for the match: "It is not for a believing man or a believing woman, when a matter has been decided by Allah and His messenger, to have any say in their decision; and whosoever disobeys Allah and His messenger has most clearly gone astray" (surah 33:36).

Zainab had no choice but to comply with Allah and his message and marry Zayd.

Several months after the marriage, Muhammed visited the home of Zayd and Zainab. Zayd was away, but Zainab invited Muhammed to enter. He turned away from her, muttering, "Praise be to God who directs our hearts." Later she told Zayd what had occurred and he immediately went to Muhammed.

"O Prophet, my father and mother are your ransom. Perhaps you like Zainab. I can leave her."

Muhammed replied to Zayd, "Hold on to your wife."

Zayd insisted, "O Messenger of God, I can leave her," to which Muhammed replied, "Keep your wife."

Later, however, Muhammed fell in a trance and received a revelation from Allah informing him that Zayd should divorce Zainab and that Muhammed had permission to marry her. Muhammed took this to mean that Allah wanted them to be married to show that adopted sons should not have the same rights as biological sons according to Islamic law.

> And remember when you said to him whom Allah had been gracious and on whom you also had conferred favors: Keep your wife to yourself and fear Allah, and you, of course, concealed that in your mind which Allah had determined to discover; and you indeed fear men, whereas it was just that you should fear Allah. But when Zayd had determined the matter [concerning Zainab] and had resolved to divorce her, we joined her in marriage to you, lest a crime should be charged on the true believers in marrying of their wives of their adopted sons, when they have determined a matter concerning them, and the command of Allah is to be performed. (surah 33:37)

When Zayd divorced his wife and Muhammed married Zainab, she was thirty-five, and Muhammed was fifty-eight. Zainab was known for her generosity, especially to the poor.

Juwairiyah Bint Al-Harith

Juwairiyah was only twenty years old when her life was turned upside down. She was the daughter of Al-Harith, the chief of the tribe Banu Mustaliq, whom Muhammed suddenly attacked. They were unprepared, and the results were devastating, especially for Juwairiyah, who became both a widow and a prisoner of war. She could die, live as a slave, or plead for her freedom before Muhammed. Juwairiyah finally met with Muhammed and Aishah, who immediately disliked Juwairiyah because she was beautiful.

Juwairiyah informed Muhammed that a certain man was willing to set her free for the sum of nine ounces of gold. She pleaded with Muhammed to accept the offer for her freedom. Muhammed, however, gave her another option. Attracted by her beauty, Muhammed offered to set her and all the captives of her tribe free and send them home if she would marry him. Juwairiyah accepted the offer and married Muhammed when she was twenty and he was fifty-eight. Muhammed kept his promise and freed more than one hundred prisoners. The marriage lasted for six years, until Muhammed died.

Ramlah Bint Abu Sufyan

Ramlah was the daughter of Abu Sufyan, an idol-worshiping leader in Mecca who bitterly opposed Islam. Although her given name was Ramlah, she was known as Umm Habiba, "mother of Habiba." Habiba was born while Ramlah was married to Ubaidullah. She and her husband embraced Islam during its early stage in Mecca and soon fled to Abyssinia. While they were living in Abyssinia, Ubaidullah turned to Christianity, but his wife held fast to her Islamic beliefs. Stories differ over whether Umm Habiba then left her husband because of his apostasy or she was widowed.

Muhammed heard that Umm Habiba was alone in Abyssinia and sent someone to propose to her on his behalf. There was an immediate wedding and a wedding feast in Abyssinia, although Muhammed was an exile in Medina and Umm Habiba couldn't leave Abyssinia for fear of encountering the enemies of her new husband from Mecca. Six years after their marriage, Umm Habiba was able to join Muhammed in Medina, and they were together four years until his death.

While Umm Habiba was married to Muhammed, her father came to visit her. He wanted to sit where Muhammed slept, but his daughter would not allow him and removed the blanket that was lying on the floor. Hurt and angry, her father left, but in the end he accepted Islam and was reconciled to his daughter.

Safiyya Bint Huyayy

Safiyya became a spoil of war after the battle of Khaybar, in which the Muslims defeated the Jewish tribe of Banu Nadir. Safiyya was the daughter of the their chief leader, Huyayy.

Safiyya had lost her husband in the war and was a seventeen-year-old slave when she appeared before Muhammed with her cousin. As an act of kindness to her in her anguish, Muhammed took off his cloak and placed it on her. He promised to give her great honor if she married him and converted to Islam.

Safiyya was of the tribe of Levi and was looked down upon as a Jewess by the other wives. One of her servants complained to a Muslim leader that Safiyya still kept the Sabbath and followed Jewish law, but Muhammed was convinced that his wife was sincere in following Islam. Safiyya and Muhammed were married for four years until he died.

Maymuna Bint Al-Harith

Maymuna was a distant relative of Muhammed. She first married a man named Mas'ud, who divorced her, and then Abdu-Ruhman, but he died. She wanted to marry Muhammed and sent someone to speak to him on her behalf. Soon after Muhammed heard of Maymuna's interest, he received a revelation from Allah: "Any believing woman who dedicates herself to the Prophet if the Prophet wishes to wed her, that is only for thee and not for the believers" (surah 33:50). Upon receiving the revelation, Muhammed took Maymuna for his wife. She was thirty-six and he was sixty.

Maymuna was known as a humble and gentle peacemaker and arbiter. She lived with Muhammed for three years until he died.

The Servant Maria Al-Kibtia

Muhammed received two servant girls as a gift from the king of Egypt. One was Maria al-Kibtia. Some Muslims say that Muhammed married her; others contend that she remained a slave mistress.

Muhammed received a revelation from Allah that forbade him to marry any more women but allowed him to have sex with and replace his servants: "It is not lawful for you [O Muhammed, to marry more] women after this, nor to exchange them for other wives, even though their beauty is pleasing to you, except those whom your right hand possesses [maidservants]; and Allah is always watching over everything" (surah 33:52).

Maria gave birth to a son that Muhammed named Ibrahim, but the child died when he was eighteen months old.

CONCLUSION

As a woman who was born and raised in Islam until I embraced the Living Savior four years ago, I cannot help but contrast the God of the *Qur'an* and the God of the Bible. Allah of the *Qur'an* gave permission for Muhammed to marry wife after wife after wife. He even allowed Muhammed's adopted son, Zayd, to divorce his wife so that Muhammed could marry her. As if that were not enough, Allah gave Muhammed permission to be intimate with his maidservants.

Then I look at the God of the Bible:

In Genesis 2:24, God says, "For this reason a man will leave his father and mother and be united to his wife, and they will become one flesh" (NIV). God repeats these words in Matthew 19:5, Mark 10:7, and Ephesians 5:31. Clearly the God of the Bible intended marriage to be two partners, a husband and a wife, and He declares marriage to be holy and sacred. He compares our relationship with Him to the loving bond between a husband and his bride: "'For your Maker is your husband—the LORD Almighty is His name—the Holy One of Israel is your Redeemer; he is called the God of all the earth. The LORD will call you back as if you were a wife deserted and distressed in spirit—a wife who married young, only to be rejected,' says your God" (Isaiah 54:5-6 NIV).

Marriage in the Bible is not intended only for our pleasure. It is to be a shadow of the intimacy and commitment we share with our heavenly Husband.

In Deuteronomy 17:16–17, God gives instructions to the kings that are appointed and says, "The king, moreover, must not acquire great numbers of horses for himself or make the people return to Egypt to get more of them, for the LORD has told you, 'You are not to go back that way again.' He must not take many wives, or his heart will be led astray. He must not accumulate large amounts of silver and gold" (NIV). God did not want Israel's kings to marry multiple wives, because He knew their hearts would be led astray.

As a result of my research, it is clear to me that the God of the Bible thinks differently than the god that inspired Muhammed's visions. It is clear to me that the God of the Bible sets different rules, different standards, and different purposes. Can Yahweh and Allah both really be the same God?

SOURCES FOR THE ORAL NARRATIVE TRADITION

Safiar-Rahman Al-Mubarakpuri, *The Sealed Nectar* (Riyadh, Saudi Arabia: Darussalam, 1979).

Hamdun Dagher, *The Position of Women in Islam* (Villach, Austria: Light Of Life, 1995), 129–83.

http://www.anwary-islam.com/women/m-womens_Daughters.htm#top.

http://www.prophetMuhammad.org/docs/relations01.html.

http://www.islamic-paths.org/Home/English/Muhammad/Book/Wives/ Introduction.htm.

http://www.thetruereligion.org/messengers.htm.

http://www.thewaytotruth.org/prophetmuhammad/wives.html.

http://www.anwary-islam.com/prophet-life/holly-p-2.htm.

http://www.youngmuslims.ca/online_library/books/women_in_ the_shade_of_islam/#2b.

Shahid Zafar Qasmi, *Mother's Of Believers* (Riyadh, Saudi Arabia: Darussalam, 1997).

3

AISHAH'S DAUGHTERS

Significant Women in the History of Islam

Emily Hunter McGowin

> Modern scholarship pays little attention to the important
> women in Islamic history. Chapter 2 sketched the biogra-
> phies of the "mothers of the believers." Here Emily Hunter
> McGowin discusses other female leaders in Islam and the
> roles these women played. Christians would do well to be-
> come familiar with these women, who also serve as a bridge
> of understanding into the Muslim mind-set. This chapter
> reaches beyond the caricatures and stereotypes of female
> Muslims often found in the media.

The "Mothers of the Faithful," the wives of Muhammed, are certainly
the most revered women in Islamic history. Traditionally, they are the
women exemplar for all faithful Muslims throughout history. Their
lives are, for the most part, considered worthy of emulation for their
obedience to Muhammed and their willingness to follow the will of
Allah. Yet other women also stand out as especially significant in Islamic history. One might think that a religion that has so often sup-
pressed and oppressed women would not have prominent examples
of women to spotlight in its history. Surprisingly, such is not the case.

Many extraordinary women played key roles in the rise of the Muslim empire. In fact, the sheer number of interesting women is overwhelming. This chapter will look at five examples, from among
hundreds. These women represent varying positions in early Islamic

social standing: a wife and mother, a socialite, a mystic, a theologian, and a politician. Their lives span roughly the first 650 years of Islamic history.

It is important to keep in mind that these women, more often than not, are celebrated because of their uncommon reputations. With the exception of Fatima, Muslim woman are not usually encouraged to personally model their lives on these women, who stand out because of their distinctiveness in Islamic history, not their ability to "blend in." It would be difficult, then, to relate these women of Islamic history to the Muslim women of the twenty-first century. For this reason, after a description of the life of each woman and her contribution to early Muslim society, a simple connection will be drawn to the lives of the average Muslim woman of today. This is done so that the lives of these women can serve as points of common ground in effectively sharing with the modern women of Islam.

THE WIFE AND MOTHER

Fatima (c. 604–632) is known primarily as the daughter of Muhammed and his first wife, Khadijah. She was also the dedicated wife of the fourth caliph, ʿAli bin Abu Taleb, Muhammed's cousin and adopted son, and mother of the famous Shiʾite imams and martyrs Hasan and Husain.[1]

History has left little information about Fatima's early life with Muhammed and Khadijah, except that it was austere and physically taxing. When Fatima was married to ʿAli at the age of twelve or fifteen (sources vary on her exact age), she was described as "tall and slender, sloe-eyed, with a gift for singing, . . . the most beautiful among Arabian women."[2] Although she was clearly considered a prize for ʿAli, who was twenty-three at the time, Fatima's married life remained difficult. Early Islamic historians emphasize the severity of her existence, describing their bed as "the wooly side of a sheepskin" and their pillow as "a cushion of tanned leather, filled with palm fibers."[3]

It is significant to note that Muhammed forbade ʿAli from taking a second wife while Fatima was alive, stating that whatever gave pain to his daughter vexed him as well. As a result, ʿAli indeed did not take any more wives until after the deaths of Muhammed (in 632) and Fatima a few months later. She was only twenty-eight years old when she died.

Fatima plays an important role in the Muslim sect known as the Shiʾites. Upon Muhammed's death, Fatima and ʿAli called on all faithful Muslims to pay homage to ʿAli as Muhammed's rightful successor. This created a serious conflict, because Muhammed's closest friend, Abu Bakr, was considered by most to be next in the line of succession. Only after six months and the death of Fatima did ʿAli swear allegiance to Abu Bakr in 632. Twenty-five years and two caliphs later, however, when the controversial third caliph, Uthman, was assassinated, ʿAli seized the Muslim kingdom, even opposing Aishah in his quest for power. ʿAli caused much division in Islam before his assassination in 661. By then, the followers of ʿAli had irreconcilably split from traditional Islam.

The followers of ʿAli became known as the Shiʾa or Shiʾites (shiat-u-ʿAli, lit. "party of ʿAli"). This faction of Islam claims that their imams, or spiritual leaders, are all divinely chosen and directly descended from ʿAli. For this reason, Fatima, the daughter of Muhammed and first wife of ʿAli, holds a place of great honor as "mother of the imams." Some refer to her as "the brilliant one," representative of the "primal mother figure, immaculate and sinless, the pattern of the virtuous woman." To others, "she embodies a life of dedication, suffering, and compassion."[4] With both her husband and two sons considered great martyrs of the Shiʾite faith, the depth of reverence shown for Fatima compares with that shown to the Virgin Mary by Roman Catholics.

Interestingly, Fatima is elevated to saintly status in every traditional sect of Islam, not just among the Shiʾites. In fact, A. Yusuf ʿAli, in his commentary on the Qurʾan, identified Fatima as "one of the four perfect women."[5]

For this reason, it may seem difficult for Christian women to find common ground between the daughter of Muhammed and the average Muslim woman. What, if anything, does the life of Fatima offer for reaching out to the Muslim women of today? Fatima's devotion to her father, husband, and sons is often praised as an example for faithful Muslim women. To respect and honor the men in her family, even to the detriment of her own life, is most pleasing to Allah. Yet, even the greatness of the prophet Muhammed could not guarantee the paradise of heaven in return for Fatima's earthly obedience. On his deathbed, Muhammed allegedly told Fatima, "You . . . work that which will gain you acceptance with the Lord; for verily I have no power to save you."

Most of today's Muslim women are trusting in their works or their children or their husbands to earn the blessings of Allah and the promise of eternal life. Yet, the Bible teaches that such works are empty and useless before a pure and holy God. Nothing a person does will earn the favor of the Lord. However, the glorious promise of the gospel message is that by Jesus Christ's merits and sacrifice on the cross, one can be saved. This message of salvation by grace through faith is the key to freedom for Muslim women caught in the trap of Islam's works-based religion.

THE SOCIALITE

The life of Fatima stands in stark contrast to that of her granddaughter, Sukaina bint al-Husain (d. 735). Daughter of the Shi?ite imam and martyr Husain, Sukaina was raised in Damascus, "the residence of the caliphs." Damascus was far removed from the constant political strife found in Mecca and Medina. Thus, for most of her life, Sukaina had great wealth, luxury, and indulgence.[6]

Like many women in Islamic history, Sukaina is most famous for her unrivaled beauty. Yet she was also known for her sense of humor and astute wit, along with a devious taste for practical jokes. Stories are told of Sukaina assembling poets around her, having them recite their most recent works, and then rewarding them based on her evaluation of their skill. Apparently, her elegance and taste in fashion were admired. The pious caliph Umar Ibn Abd al-Aziz is said to have severely punished several men of the city when he felt they paid too much attention to the remarkable style of Sukaina's clothing and hair.

Beyond her character and reputation, however, Sukaina's married life presents interesting insight into the powerful status of such Islamic socialites. It is well documented that Sukaina was married at least four times, with some sources claiming she had as many as six husbands of respectable social position. It is also not a secret that most, if not all, of her divorces occurred at her initiative.[7] In fact, much attention is given to her unhappy marriage to Zayd Ibn Amr, grandson of Caliph Uthman. It is said that she agreed to marry him "on the condition that he would never repudiate [divorce] her on his initiative, nor touch another woman, nor refuse her anything she wished, allow her to live where she wanted, and not contradict her in anything."[8] It is, then, no surprise that "the two often quarreled."

It was not uncommon for Sukaina and her current husband to come before the judges for arbitration of a marital dispute. Apparently, Sukaina's provocative tongue so enraged one judge that he threatened her, stating, "If you were not a [gentle] woman, I would have you whipped!" Sukaina's contempt for her husbands caused many of the men present at these proceedings to fear that their own wives might take up her abusive ways. Few men were willing to brave Sukaina's humiliating and painful assaults, to enjoy her celebrated beauty, wealth, and intellect.

From the life of Sukaina it is clear that the possession of vast wealth and political power, even in the early Muslim society, was enough to allow for female defiance of otherwise oppressive rules and standards. Most Muslim women today would not dare to treat their husbands with such disrespect, for fear of their husband's reprimand and the often severe punishment of their community.

Although few Muslim women have the prerogative to behave in defiance of their husbands and the rules of the Qur'an and Hadith, that does not necessarily mean that the desire to do so is gone. Apart from the love of Jesus Christ, every soul is in bondage to the oppressive power of sin and this bondage is vividly seen in the lives of most Muslim women. Though many such women may believe that their spiritual bondage will end with the reform of Islam and Islamic law,

the reality is that without Christ, there is no true freedom. The longing in these women's souls for liberty can only find authentic fulfillment in the forgiveness of Christ and the promises of Scripture.

The power of God that enabled the apostle Paul to endure the Roman prisons is the same power that can enable today's Muslim women
to find their soul's greatest fulfillment in Christ and to persevere in
and against the chains of Islam.

THE MYSTIC

While Sukaina carried on a life of pampered luxury in Damascus,
the famous Sufi mystic Rabiʾa al-ʿAdawiyya (c. 717–801) was model-
ing asceticism and self-discipline. The following has been written of
her: "Veiled with a special veil . . . burned up in love and longing . . .
accepted among men, Rabiʾa ʿAdawiyya—the mercy of God Most High
upon her. . . . When a woman is a man on the path of the lord Most
High, she cannot be called woman."[9]

Rabiʾa al-ʿAdawiyya is said to have been born to a poor Muslim
couple as the last of four daughters (Rabiʾa means "the fourth one").
When her parents died suddenly, Rabiʾa was separated from her sisters and sold to a "wicked master." One night, in despair at her cruel
treatment, Rabiʾa supposedly cried out to heaven, saying, "All I need is
for you to be pleased with me, to know whether you are pleased with
me or not." According to legend, she then heard a voice respond, "Do
not be sad. Tomorrow a grandeur will be yours such that the closest of
the heavenly company will take pride in you."

This encounter with deity was said to be the first of many for the
woman who would be called "the friend of God." Once Rabiʾa's harsh
master released her from servitude, she began a long commitment to
a life of contemplation, meditation, worship, and service to Allah. She
became famous for her contempt of the material world and her un-
swerving devotion to the ascetic and simple life. Sufi masters of the
day came from all over to consult with Rabiʾa, seeking her knowledge
that was, as one admirer stated, "untaught and unheard, coming down
to [the] heart without the intermediary of any creature."[10] Popular

tales of Rabiʾa's life include miracle stories, such as the raising of her dead mule to life in a barren desert.

In addition to these extraordinary spiritual characteristics, Rabiʾa possessed a unique place in Islamic society. Her status as an orphan and a freed slave allowed her the right to refuse the offers of marriage that came from numerous suitors, apparently because no male authority governed her life. As a result, she remained a single woman until her death and was permitted a measure of autonomy in her extensive travel and nomadic habitation that married women simply did not possess.[11] So, although Rabiʾa often spoke of herself as a "weak woman," it is obvious that she maintained unparalleled power compared to the majority of women throughout Islamic history.

The life, fame, and honor given to Rabiʾa al-ʿAdawiyya certainly defies the standards and stereotypes of the role of women laid out in the *Qurʾan, Hadith,* and modern-day *shariʾa* law (see chapters 4 and 5). The life of this saintly mystic holds little in common with that of Muslim women of the twenty-first century. However, consider the reason Rabiʾa gave for not marrying:

> I am dismayed with care over three things. If you free me of these cares, I'll take a husband. First, at the moment of death, will my faith be sound or not? Second, will they put the book of my deeds in my right hand or not?[12] Third, which group will I be in on that hour when they lead a group to the right to paradise and a group to the left to hell? . . . With such anguish before me, how can I be concerned with taking a husband?[13]

It is clear that Rabiʾa was plagued with desperate uncertainty about her eternal destiny. This doubt of Allah's final judgment has pervaded the life and culture of Muslims since the days of Muhammed. Even the saintly Rabiʾa, the "friend of God," was in anguish that Allah would not accept her. How much more must the average Muslim woman fear the coming judgment of Allah? As Christians reach out to Muslim women, this point of sensitivity to the gospel message has not changed. The eternal security offered by Jesus Christ and the certainty of the hope we have is of special significance when speaking to Islamic women about our faith.

THE THEOLOGIAN

In 763, about fifty years after the birth of Rabiʾa, another great female intellectual was born in the Muslim holy city of Mecca. Nafisa was the great-granddaughter of Hasan, who was the grandson of Muhammed. She was raised in Medina but later traveled to Egypt with her husband (or her brother; sources differ). Almost nothing is known of Nafisa's personal life, except that her severe asceticism and generosity to the poor made her beloved and famous in the city of Cairo.

The most significant aspect of Nafisa's life, however, is her apparently vast grasp of theological matters. Her insight into the traditions of the *Qurʾan* and *Hadith* were so well respected that even the acclaimed jurist Muhammad ash-Shafiʾi, founder of the Shafiʾi school of law, visited Nafisa and listened to her instruction. The people of Egypt sought her out to answer questions about life and to arbitrate complaints.

The boldness of this female theologian is apparent in one story: "When people complained to her about the injustice of the Egyptian governor of that time, she is said to have stood in his path and handed him a note in which she accused him of tyranny and called on him to be more just."[14] Surely this unique woman proved a daunting force in Egypt's capital city, particularly with the common people so fiercely loyal to her. When Nafisa died in 824, she was buried in Cairo at the request of the local people. The mausoleum erected in her honor became famous as "a place where prayers were heard by God."

Nafisa was an exceptional woman who gained acceptance in male-dominated Muslim society. How can a Muslim woman in today's world, usually discouraged from seeking education and spiritual knowledge, begin to relate to this Egyptian Islamic saint? It is widely recognized in most faiths that women, as a whole, tend to be very open and emotionally sensitive to matters of spirituality. Although Nafisa was misguided in the object of her devotion, most women share her earnest desire to search out the truths of God. Thus, as Christian women seek to share the God of the Bible with Muslim women, they can usually count on a heartfelt sensitivity to the gospel message. The power of the Holy Spirit is ultimately responsible for the conviction and conversion of a soul, but a Christian woman can at least recognize an inherent sympathy in her Muslim friend in her desire to know the one true God.

THE POLITICIAN

Many Muslims would not like to have a woman ruler or political leader. Although the *Qurʾan* mentions the legendary Queen of Sheba without censure, the *Hadith* contains several admonitions against the rule of women over men. Nevertheless, rare women have ascended to high office in unusual situations. Although considered rogues in their positions, these women for the most part maintained power on the level of male rulers, with their own ruthless cruelty.

Roughly two hundred years after the death of Nafisa, one such Islamic woman arrived on the scene. Shajarat ad-Durr (d. 1250) was the Turkish slave of the Egyptian Ayyubid ruler al-Malik as-Salih, but she became his wife after bearing him a son. Following the arrival of the Crusaders of Louis IX (1214–1270) in Damietta, a city in the Nile Delta on the Mediterranean Coast, Shajarat ad-Durr's husband died. His only son and successor, Turanshah, was murdered shortly thereafter. To stabilize a perilous political situation, Shajarat ad-Durr assumed the title of sultana on May 2, 1250, and retained rule until July 30 of that year.

As was the custom, her subjects declared their allegiance to her, she signed decrees as sultan and, as ruler, she was the subject of Friday prayers. In addition, coins were circulated bearing her name—the first coins minted with the name of a woman in more than six hundred years of Islamic history. A Syrian historian of the day said of her, "She was a Turk, the most cunning woman of her age, unmatched in beauty among women and in determination among men."[15]

Only a few days after the sultana assumed power, Damietta came back under Muslim control and an oath of allegiance to the sultana was demanded from the Syrians, particularly the viceroy, who had joined with Egypt in its fight against the Crusaders. An intense dispute broke out over this issue, with the decision finally being made to remove Shajarat ad-Durr from power and marry her to Aybak, supreme commander of the Egyptian armed forces. This seemed to placate the Syrian leaders, but history relates that the struggle between Egypt and Syria only increased. It appears from Oriental historians that Shajarat ad-Durr retained power as sultana, issuing imperial decrees that were obeyed by the people. There is evidence that she continued to be addressed as sultana. One historian offers a simple explanation for this peculiarity: "She dominated [her husband], and he had nothing to say."[16]

This imbalance of power was complicated when Shajarat ad-Durr discovered that her new husband intended to acquire another wife. Infuriated at the possible threat to her power and position, she had Aybak murdered. Unfortunately, she had not secured a proper successor to Aybak, and the rioting that ensued resulted in the crucifixion of the murderers. History does not reveal exactly how Shajarat ad-Durr died, but we are told that in the aftermath of the violent uproar, "[her] half-naked body was found in the moat of the citadel."[17]

The life of Shajarat ad-Durr reveals a tragic, albeit dramatic, side to an Islamic woman's involvement in the intrigues of politics. Although Muslim women were rarely permitted into such arenas of power, those who did achieve a measure of authority were quick to adopt the brutal and deceitful tactics necessary to succeed. Their political tactics were often more treacherous than those of their male counterparts. Nonetheless, although Muslim women, as a whole, have been oppressed by men, when the tables have turned the women possessed within themselves the ability for great wickedness. The Bible speaks to this truth when it states, "All have sinned and fall short of the glory of God" (Romans 3:23 NIV). We must recognize and vigorously seek to end the harsh reality of Islamic women's dreadful plight around the world. At the same time, we must realize the truth that all are sinners and must repent.

There is no true good news without true bad news. The bad news for Muslim women is that they are sinners who have offended a holy God and broken their relationship with Him. The good news, of course, is that they have a Savior, Jesus Christ, who has taken the penalty for their sins and seeks to save them from eternal punishment. This same Savior can seal them with the Holy Spirit of God, who will work in them to bring more abundant life in the power of Christ. This is the truth that every Muslim woman, rich or poor, great or small, young or old, desperately needs to hear.

CONCLUSION

Many women have distinguished themselves in Islamic history. Though they are not often written about or highly publicized, hundreds of women have played key roles in the spread of the Muslim faith around the world, despite the very real restrictions placed on them by the standards of the *Qur'an*, *Hadith*, and *shari'a* law. These women defied authorities and rules of the day. They stand out against the expansive backdrop of Islam's male-dominated religion.

The other side of this story, however, is not quite so romantic. For every Muslim woman who has risen above suffering and degradation, a million others have not had that advantage. If we suppose that half of the 1.2 billion Muslims on the globe today are women, there are at least 500 million Muslim women, most of whom have never heard of Sukaina, Rabi'a, or the other famous women. They are the true "voices behind the veil" who cannot put a face to the longings and desires of their souls because of the restrictions and dreadful injustices inflicted upon them.

Yet, there is a ray of hope. The truths revealed in the lives of these women from the past remain true in the lives of Muslim women of the twenty-first century. Like Fatima, they cannot trust in their works and good deeds to earn favor with God. Like Sukaina, their sorrow and desire for freedom can only be truly satisfied in the saving grace of Jesus Christ. Like Rabi'a, they long for security in their eternal destiny, which is ever elusive in the religion of Islam. Like Nafisa, they are remarkably open and sensitive to the spiritual truths offered by the Word of God. And, like Shajarat ad-Durr, they desperately need the cleansing power of the Savior to forgive their sins and give them new and abundant life, both in this age and in the age to come.

May the lessons learned from these amazing women of Islamic history prove useful today as Christians faithfully and patiently share the truths of Christ with contemporary Muslim women.

NOTES

1. Shiʾite Muslims would not consider ʿAli the fourth caliph, because they negate the earthly rule of the caliphate and emphasize instead the spiritual rule of the divinely chosen imams. Thus, Shiʾites would consider ʿAli the first imam, a divinely inspired intermediary between man and Allah.

2. Robert Payne, *The History of Islam* (New York: Dorset, 1987), 32.

3. Wiebke Walther, *Women in Islam* (New York: Markus Wiener, 1993), 108.

4. John L. Esposito, *Islam: The Straight Path* (Oxford: Oxford University Press, 1991), 112.

5. A. Yusuf ʿAli, *Holy Qurʾan: Text, Translation, and Commentary* (Brentwood, Md.: Amana, 1983), n. 1573. The other three "perfect women" are Mary, the mother of Jesus; Khadijah, the wife of Muhammed; and ʿAsiya, the wife of the Pharaoh, who ʿAli suspects is the same woman who saved the life of the baby Moses.

6. The above information and the majority of the following research are from Walther, *Women in Islam*, 112–14.

7. Leila Ahmed, *Women and Gender in Islam* (New Haven, Conn.: Yale University Press, 1993), 77.

8. Walther, *Women in Islam*, 113.

9. The above excerpt and the following research are taken from the work, Michael A. Sells, ed. and trans., *Early Islamic Mysticism: Sufi, Qurʾan, MiʾRaj, Poetic, and Theological Writings* (New York: Paulist, 1996), 151–70. Sells, in turn, makes use of the English translation by Paul Losensky of the Persian work, *Memorial of the Friends of God*, by the Sufi writer and poet, Faridu d-Din ʿAttar (d. ca. 627/1230). See also Walther, *Women in Islam*, 109, and Ahmed, *Women and Gender in Islam*, 96–98.

10. Sells, *Early Islamic Mysticism*, 151–70.

11. Ibid., 96-98, for discussion of this rare situation.

12. Sells explains this statement with the following explanation: "The *Qurʾan* refers to the moment of truth or day of judgment when those whose book (of deeds in their lifetime) is given to them. Those who are given the book in the right hand or who are led off to the right are given the garden. Those whose book is given into the left hand or are led off to the left are those who are given the fire."

13. Sells, *Early Islamic Mysticism*, 162.

14. Walther, *Women in Islam*, 110.

15. Ibid., 120.

16. Ibid., 121.

17. Ibid.

4

THE *QUR'AN*, THE *HADITH*, AND WOMEN

Diana L. Owen

When the average Christian reads the *Qur'an*, many verses seem to be vague and confusing. Rather than providing a Christian commentary on the Qur'anic text, Diana L. Owen has examined the commentary of prominent Muslim scholar Abdullah Yusuf 'Ali. In this chapter, she provides a systematic study of Islamic teaching on women in six distinct categories. She also includes supplemental teachings from the *Hadith*, to illustrate simply the intricacy of Islamic theology. For the sake of accuracy, this chapter will include both the title and the chronological number of each surah. See Appendix for a complete list of the Qur'anic chapters. This is a vital chapter to provide an overview of a complex topic within Islam.

The *Qur'an* and the *Hadith* are the two most authoritative sacred texts of Islam. The *Qur'an* contains the revelation of Allah given to Muhammed through the angel Gabriel. The *Hadith* is a multivolume collection of the teachings and sayings of Muhammed.

The purpose of this chapter is to survey a limited number of topics within the *Qur'an* and the *Hadith* that concern women—creation, parity/disparity, marriage, divorce, sexual immorality, and life after death.

Rather than presenting various interpretations of a text by Islamic scholars, this survey will allow the text to speak for itself, including only the commentary given by the respected translator and commentator Abdullah Yusuf ʿAli. For easier understanding of the *Qurʾan*, the reader must take into consideration those words (shown in brackets [ ]) that have been added to the text.

THE DOCTRINE OF CREATION

Do Muslims believe in a creation by divine fiat, as do orthodox Christians? The *Qurʾan* speaks explicitly of Allah's formation of the earth, specifically proclaiming in surah 16 an-Nahl that all of the earth gives Allah glory. This act of creation is demonstrated in the *Qurʾan*, but with some distinct differences from the biblical record.

The Announcement

> Behold, thy Lord said to the angels: "I will create a vicegerent on earth." They said: "Wilt Thou place therein one who will make mischief therein and shed blood?—Whilest we do celebrate Thy praises and glorify Thy holy [name]? He said: "I know what ye know not." (surah 2:30)

Why would the angels question Allah? According to Abdullah Yusuf ʾAli, the angels were holy and pure, but lacked the passion or emotion to allow them to wholly know Allah's nature.[1]

Why would Allah create humanity if he already had angels who praised and glorified him? ʿAli continues,

> If man was to be endued with emotions, those emotions could lead him to the highest and drag him to the lowest. The power of will or choosing would have to go with them, in order that man might steer his own bark. This power of will gave him to some extent a mastery over his own fortunes and over nature, thus bringing him nearer to the God-like nature, which has

supreme master and will. . . . The perfect vicegerent is he who
has the power of initiative himself, but whose independent
action always reflects perfectly the will of his Principal. . . .
The angels . . . perhaps they also, being without emotions, did
not understand the whole of Allah's nature, which gives and
asks for love.[2]

It would appear, then, that Allah was creating man that he might
have a relationship with him; relationship being the context within
which love is given and received. And yet, although al-Hashr (surah
59) describes Allah as "Most Gracious, Most Merciful . . . the Sovereign, the Holy One, the Source of Peace [and Perfection], the Guardian of Faith, the Preserver of Safety, the Exalted in Might, the Irresistible,
the Supreme," for most Muslims the relationship is that of "servant to
master; Allah is a distant sovereign."[3]

The Creation of Human Beings

Behold! thy Lord said to the angels: "I am about to create man,
from sounding clay from mud moulded into shape; when I
have fashioned him [in due proportion] and breathed into
him of My spirit, fall ye down in obeisance unto him." (surah
15:28–29)

And He taught Adam the names of all things. . . . (surah 2:31)

The creation of human beings was a process. The physical body
was, according to theologians, "formed from wet clay moulded into
shape and then dried until it could emit sound."[4] Allah "fashioned
him in due proportions, giving him extraordinary capacities, and the
means wherewith he can fulfil his high destiny."[5] When Allah taught
humankind the names of things, or "the inner nature and qualities of
things . . . feelings . . . which were outside the nature of angels," he
enabled people "to love and understand love, and thus plan and ini-
tiate."[6] "Having given [to humanity] a limited free will,"[7] Allah also

gave to the human makeup "a just bias" (surah 82:7). Once completed, this creature's status was raised higher than the angels, who had been created "from the fire of a scorching wind" (surah 15:27). Thus, the angels were expected to bow down before humanity."[8]

The Creation of Woman

"It is He Who created you from a single person, and made his mate of like nature, in order that he might dwell with her [in love]." (surah 7:189)

The Prophet said, ". . . And I advise you to take care of the women, for they are created from a rib." (hadith 7.62.114)

According to this hadith, Muhammed said that the woman was created from a rib, but this is not the mode recorded in the *Qur'an*. Instead of being made *from* man, woman was made *in the likeness* of man. She had "attributes, capacities, predilections, and dispositions," which were like those of man, and therefore, she had the "same moral and religious rights and duties."[9]

Dwelling in the Garden

We said: "O Adam! dwell thou and thy wife in the Garden: and eat of the bountiful things therein as [where and when] ye will; but approach not this tree, or ye run into harm and transgression." (surah 2:35)

After Allah created man and woman, he placed them in the Garden. The Garden, according to ʿAli, was not a place on the earth. He says that one "must suppose Man to be on another plane altogether— of felicity, innocence, trust, a spiritual existence, with the negation of enmity, want of faith, and all evil."[10]

Man and woman were given permission to eat at their leisure of all that was in the Garden except that food that was on a specific tree.

When eating that which was permissible, they experienced "enjoyment generally, physical, social, mental and moral, and spiritual."[11]

The Fall

> Then began Satan to whisper suggestions to them, in order to reveal to them their shame that was hidden from them [before]: he said: "Your Lord only forbade you this tree, lest ye should become angels or such beings as live forever." And he swore to them both, that he was their sincere adviser. (Surah al-Aʿraf 7:20–21)

> Then did Satan make them slip from the [Garden], and get them out of the state [of felicity] in which they had been. We said: "Get ye down, all [ye people], with enmity between yourselves. On earth will be your dwelling place and your means of livelihood—for a time." Then learnt Adam from his Lord words of inspiration, and his Lord turned towards him; for He is Oft-Returning, Most Merciful. We said: "Get ye down all from here: And if, as is sure, there comes to you guidance from Me, whosoever follows My guidance, on them shall be no fear, nor shall they grieve." (Surah al-Baqarah 2:36–38)

When Allah created man and woman, they were "innocent in matters material as well as spiritual," and they "knew no evil."[12] The single quality, a limited faculty of choice, which raised them above the angels, "also implied that they had the capacity of evil, which by the training of their own will, they were to reject."[13]

ʿAli believes that the word used to describe the fall, or *slip*, of man and woman "denotes the idea of Evil gradually tempting man from a higher to a lower state."[14] Allah had told them that Satan, who had refused to bow down to man, "was an avowed enemy" (surah 7:22), and yet, they chose to succumb to the wiles of Satan and ate that which was forbidden to them.

According to surah 7:11–12, Iblis (Satan) refused to bow down be-fore people because he felt that being made from fire instead of clay, he was their superior. Iblis was cursed by Allah; he was "deprived of Allah's Grace and became in the spiritual world what an outlaw is in a political kingdom."[15] "Iblis (the Rebellious) is powerless against Allah. He turns therefore against man and becomes Satan (the Enemy)."[16]

It should be noted that "the theory of fallen angels is not accepted in Muslim theology."[17] In order to alleviate the appearance of contra-diction, Islam holds to two categories of supernatural beings: (1) *angels*, who do not have free will; (2) *jinn*, who have free will.

As a result of their disobedience, the man and woman were ex-pelled from the Garden and sent to dwell on the earth.[18] Recognizing that they had erred, they made an effort to learn from Allah words of inspiration, or "spiritual knowledge."[19] Allah, in turn, had mercy on them and gave them the assurance of his guidance, which if followed would free them "from fear for the present or the future, and any grief or sorrow for the past" and allow them to grow nearer to Allah.[20]

THE DOCTRINE OF GENDER PARITY AND DISPARITY

If Allah created men and women, are they also on level ground before Allah? Islamic doctrine teaches a caste system between the sexes. This doctrine is different from the traditional categories of Christian distinction. In Christian theological discussions there are two views regarding what the Bible teaches about the roles of men and women. The position of *egalitarianism* sees no distinction in gender roles. *Complementarianism* views the genders as equal in value, but distinct in role and authority structure. Emir Mehmet Caner, a former Muslim and the general editor of this volume, coined the corresponding phrase *"Islamic disciplinarianism"* to describe the protective stance that males take over females in the Muslim world. Their position comes from clear teachings within the *Qur'an* and the *Hadith*.

A Matter of Genetics

And women shall have rights similar to the rights against them, according to what is equitable; but men have a degree [of advantage] over them. (Surah al-Baqarah 2:228)

Get two witnesses, out of your own men, and if there are not two men, then a man and two women, such as ye choose, for witnesses, so that if one of them errs, the other can remind her. (Surah al-Baqarah 2:282)

I have not seen anyone more deficient in intelligence and religion than you. (hadith 2.24.541)

The Prophet said, "Isn't the witness of a woman equal to half of that of a man?" The women said, "Yes." He said, "This is because of the deficiency of a woman's mind." (hadith 3.48.826)

Although the woman was made in the likeness of man, she was not placed on an equal plane with him. According to the *Qur'an*, the woman is subordinate to man (Surah al-Baqarah 2:228). When commenting on this verse, ʿAli states that "the difference in economic position between the sexes makes the man's rights and liabilities a *little* greater than the woman's," but his explanation appears to contradict other verses recorded in the *Qur'an* and *Hadith*.[21] In the *Hadith*, Muhammed explains that the reason the woman is not equal to the man is a matter of genetics—a deficient mind or intelligence.

Receiving an Inheritance

Allah [thus] directs you as regards your children's [inheritance]: to the male, a portion equal to that of two females: if only daughters, two or more, their share is two-thirds of the inheritance; if only one, her share is a half. (Surah an-Nisa 4:11)

The Prophet said, "Give the *Fara'id* [the shares of the inheritance that are prescribed in the *Qur'an*] to those who are entitled to receive it; and whatever is left should be given to the closest male relative of the deceased." (hadith 8.80.738)

Only a portion of the formula used in the disbursement of an inheritance has been included, but the exhaustive formula, which is found in surah 4:11–12 and 4:176, appears to be quite complicated. According to 'Ali, "Muslim jurists have collected a vast amount of learning on this subject, and this body of law is enough by itself to form the subject of lifelong study."[22] The reality that a woman does not receive an inheritance equal to a man, solely because of her gender, is quite clear.

THE DOCTRINE OF MARRIAGE

How is the process of marriage different in Islam from Christianity? If the male is designed to discipline the female, does the female have any voice in the choice of a mate, or any rights in the marital union? The *Qur'an* speaks more to men than to women in this instance, but the woman has some procedures to follow if she is wronged.

The Selection of a Wife

Do not marry unbelieving women until they believe: a slave woman who believes is better than an unbelieving woman, even though she allure you. Nor marry [your daughters] to unbelievers until they believe: a man slave who believes is better than an unbeliever, even though he allure you. (Surah al-Baqarah 2:221)

Prohibited to you [for marriage] are—Your mothers, daughters, sisters; father's sisters, mother's sisters; brother's daughters, sister's daughters; foster-mothers (who gave you suck), foster-sisters; your wives' mothers; your step-daughters under your guardianship, born of your wives to whom ye have gone in—no prohibition if ye have not gone in—[those who have been] wives of your sons proceeding from your loins; and two sisters in wedlock at one and the same time, except for what is past; for Allah is Oft-forgiving, Most Merciful— Also [prohibited are] women already married, except those whom your right hands possess: thus hath Allah ordained [prohibitions] against you: except for these, all others are lawful. (Surah al-Nisa 4:23–24)

[Lawful unto you in marriage are not only] chaste women who are believers, but chaste women among the People of the Book. (Surah al-Ma'idah 5:5)

Marry those among you who are single, or the virtuous ones among your slaves, male or female: if they are in poverty, Allah will give them means out of His grace: for Allah encompasseth all, and He knoweth all things. (Surah an-Naur 24:32)

I asked the Prophet, "O Allah's Apostle! Should the women be asked for their consent to their marriage?" He said, "Yes." (hadith 9.85.79)

Since Allah created mates to "dwell in tranquility" and "put love and mercy between [their] (hearts)" (Surah al-Rum 30:21), one would assume that he would also create guidelines to assist in finding one's mate. Recorded in Surah an-Nisa 4:23–24 is a detailed list of relatives whom one is prohibited from marrying. For the most part, this list would be endorsed by Western society.

According to Surah an-Naur 24:32, it is permissible for one to marry a slave. One could speculate that this was a means to better the life of a slave, because Muhammed said, "Any man who has a slave girl whom he educates properly, teaches good manners, manumits [liberates] and marries her, will get a double reward" (hadith 7.62.20).

Thus far the guidelines are clear, but there appears to be a contradiction in the *Qur'an* concerning the marrying of an unbeliever. Surah al-Baqarah 2:221 states that neither a man nor a woman is to marry an unbeliever. According to ʿAli, the reason for this is that "if religion is at all a real influence in life to both parties or to either party, a difference in this vital matter must affect the lives of both more profoundly than differences of birth, race, language, or position in life. It is therefore only right that the parties to be married should have the same spiritual outlook. If two persons love each other, their outlook in the highest things of life must be the same."[23]

The contradiction surfaces in Surah al-Ma'idah 5:5, which states that a man is allowed to marry a woman among People of the Book—Jews and Christians. By definition, a Christian or a Jew is not a believer in the tenets of Islam. ʿAli's explanation of the verse appears to justify "missionary dating" for men but not for women:

> Islam is not exclusive. Social intercourse, including intermarriage, is permitted with the People of the Book. A Muslim man may marry a woman from their ranks on the same terms as he would marry a Muslim woman. . . . A Muslim woman may not marry a non-Muslim man, because her Muslim status would be affected: the wife ordinarily takes the nationality and status given by her husband's law. A non-Muslim marrying a Muslim husband would be expected eventually to accept Islam. Any man or woman, of any race or faith, may, on accepting Islam, freely marry any Muslim woman or man, provided it be from motives of purity and chastity and not of lewdness.[24]

The union of a man and a woman should only occur with the consent of both individuals (hadith 7.62.20). Unfortunately, in a society with arranged marriages, the bride's disapproval is not always considered.

The Wife as a Possession

Your wives are as a tilth [field] unto you; so approach your
tilth when or how ye will. (Surah al-Baqarah 2:223)

Fair in the eyes of men is the love of things they covet: women
and sons; heaped-up hoards of gold and silver; horses branded
[for blood and excellence]; and [wealth of] cattle and well-
tilled land. Such are the possessions of this world's life. (Surah
al-ʿImran 3:14)

The Prophet said, "A woman is married for four things, i.e.,
her wealth, her family status, her beauty and her religion."
(hadith 7.62.27)

The Prophet said, "If a man invites his wife to sleep with him
and she refuses to come to him, then the angels send their
curses on her till morning." (hadith 7.62.121)

The denigration of women, who allegedly are genetically inferior
to men, continues within the context of marriage. A woman is an object, a possession, which is coveted by man (Surah al-ʿImran 3:14).
She is likened to a field, and her husband, as landowner, is permitted
to approach her at his leisure in order to satiate his appetite (Surah al-
Baqarah 2:223). According to Muhammed, should a wife refuse to have
sexual relations with her husband, she will be cursed (hadith 7.62.121).

The Responsibility of a Wife

The righteous women are devoutly obedient, and guard in
[the husband's] absence what Allah would have them guard.
(Surah an-Nisa 4:34)

Allah's Apostle said, "Surely! Everyone of you is a guardian
and is responsible for his charges: The Imam [ruler] of the

ɔle is a guardian and is responsible for his subjects; a man is the guardian of his family [household] and is responsible for his subjects; a woman is the guardian of her husband's home and of his children and is responsible for them; and the slave of a man is a guardian of his master's property and is responsible for it. Surely, everyone of you is a guardian and responsible for his charges." (hadith 9.89.252)

The Prophet said: "I was shown the Hell-fire and that the majority of its dwellers were women who were ungrateful." It was asked, "Do they disbelieve in Allah?" (or, "Are they ungrateful to Allah?") He replied, "They are ungrateful to their husbands and are ungrateful for the favors and the good (charitable deeds) done to them." (hadith 1.2.28)

If a woman in Islam wishes to be considered righteous and to be found worthy of paradise, she must fulfill the duties that have been given her as a wife. According to the *Qur'an*, a wife is to be obedient to her husband and to "guard in [her husband's] absence" (Surah an-Nisa 4.34). Speaking to this text, ʿAli states that it may also be rendered "and protect [the husband's interests] in his absence, as Allah has protected them."[25] He continues to comment on the text, giving two interpretations:

If we take the rendering as in the text, the meaning is: the good wife is obedient and harmonious in her husband's presence, and in his absence guards his reputation and property and her own virtue, as ordained by Allah. If we take the rendering as in the note, we reach the same result in a different way: the good wife, in her husband's absence, remembering how Allah has given her a sheltered position, does everything to justify that position by guarding her own virtue and his reputation and property.[26]

The *Hadith* further defines the responsibilities of a wife. She is "the guardian of her husband's home and of his children and is responsible for them" (9.89.252). Because she may not be the only wife in the home, the scope of her duties may not be as inclusive as those of wives in Western society. She may only be responsible for the cooking, and not for the cleaning or laundry.

Regardless of the specific duties given to her, a wife must attend to them in a manner that expresses her gratitude to her husband for his provision. For though she is a believer, according to Islam, if she is ungrateful to her husband, she will not go to paradise but to hell (hadith 1.2.28).

The Respect for a Mother

> A man came to Allah's Apostle and said, "O Allah's Apostle! Who is more entitled to be treated with the best companionship by me?" The Prophet said, "Your mother." The man said. "Who is next?" The Prophet said, "Your mother." The man further said, "Who is next?" The Prophet said, "Your mother." The man asked for the fourth time, "Who is next?" The Prophet said, "Your father." (hadith 8.73.2)

> Allah's Apostle said thrice, "Shall I not inform you of the biggest of the great sins?" We said, "Yes, O Allah's Apostle." He said, "To join partners in worship with Allah: to be undutiful to one's parents." (hadith 8.73.7)

> A man came to the Prophet asking his permission to take part in Jihad. The Prophet asked him, "Are your parents alive?" He replied in the affirmative. The Prophet said to him, "Then exert yourself in their service." (hadith 4.52.48)

Although the *Qur'an* is silent on the position of motherhood, the *Hadith* speaks very highly of it. Regardless of their ages, children are commanded to honor their mothers, treating them with the utmost of respect. A Muslim son is dismissed from his duty to participate in jihad in the event he is needed to attend to his mother (hadith 4.52.48).

The failure of children to honor their mothers is *shirk*, or very high sin [or *haram* or *kabair*]; it is second only to disbelieving in Allah.

The Disciplining of a Wife

> Men are the protectors and maintainers of women, because Allah has given the one more [strength] than the other, and because they support them from their means. Therefore the righteous women are devoutly obedient, and guard in [the husband's] absence what Allah would have them guard. As to those women on whose part ye fear disloyalty and ill conduct, admonish them [first], [next], refuse to share their beds, [and last] beat them [lightly]; but if they return to obedience, seek not against them Means [of annoyance]: For Allah is Most High, great [above you all]. (Surah an-Nisa 4:34)

Included in the responsibilities of a husband is the training of his wife, but the confines within which he is to fulfill this duty is one of the most controversial issues addressed by the *Qur²an*. In fact, there are very few texts within the *Qur²an* that receive more attention than those that deal with the beating of a wife.

Surah an-Nisa 4:34 appears to present the protocol for the discipline of a woman whose "disloyalty or ill conduct" is suspect. According to the text, the husband is permitted to admonish her, to withhold sex from her, and to beat her. Should the husband choose to withhold sex, he may do so for up to four months (Surah al-Baqarah 2:226). Should the husband decide that a beating is necessary, ʿAli added to the text in his translation, the husband is to do it "lightly." The *Hadith*, however, suggests that the beating may be very brutal. According to Muhammed, "A man will not be asked as to why he beat his wife" (Sunan Abu Dawud Hadith 11.2142).

When commenting on surah 4:34, ʿAli presents a different position concerning the means for disciplining a woman. He contends that the means listed is a series of steps:

1. Perhaps verbal advice or admonition may be sufficient.
2. If not, sex relations may be suspended.
3. If this is not sufficient, some slight physical correction may be administered.
4. If all this fails, a family council is recommended.[27]

If the discipline administered results in a woman returning to obedience, the husband is required to forgive and forget. He is forbidden to seek "against them Means [of annoyance]," which, according to 'Ali, consist of "temper, nagging, sarcasm, speaking at each other in other people's presence."[28] In fairness, recent Islamic, and especially Western Islamic, scholarship has begun to emphasize the Qur'anic and Hadithic texts that discourage the beating of the wife, such as Sahih al-Bukhari 7.72.715.

Polygamy

If ye fear that ye shall not be able to deal justly with the orphans, Marry women of your choice, Two, or three, or four; But if ye fear that ye shall not be able to deal justly [with them], then only one, or [a captive] that your right hands possess, that will be more suitable, to prevent you from doing injustice. (Surah an-Nisa 4:3)

Ye are never able to be fair and just as between women, even if it is your ardent desire: but turn not away [from a woman] altogether, so as to leave her [as it were] hanging [in the air]. (Surah an-Nisa 4:129)

Aishah said, "O my nephew! [This verse has been revealed in connection with] an orphan girl under the guardianship of her guardian who is attracted by her wealth and beauty and intends to marry her with a Mahr less than what other women of her standard deserve. So they [such guardians] have been forbidden to marry them unless they do justice to them and give them their full Mahr, and they are ordered to marry other women instead of them." (hadith 7.62.2)

Both the *Qurʾan* and the *Hadith* clearly permit the practice of polygamy. According to Surah al-Nisa 4:3, a man may have up to four wives. The permission granted, however, is conditional. A man may marry more than one wife only if he commits to treat all of his wives in an equal manner. This task, according to surah 4:129, is impossible to fulfill. Commenting on Surah an-Nisa 4:129, ʿAli states, "If, in the hope that he might be able to fulfill it, a man puts himself in that impossible position, it is only right to insist that he should not discard one but at least fulfill all the outward duties that are incumbent on him in respect of her."[29]

The practice of polygamy is, under certain circumstances, actually encouraged. Presented earlier in this chapter was Surah al-ʿImran 3:14, which shows that men covet women. Surah 4:3 speaks of a man not being able to control his desires when around orphans. It will be shown later in this chapter that fornication and adultery *(zinah)* are major sins *(kabair)*. With this in mind, it would be reasonable for one to conclude that polygamy was permitted in order that men might avoid committing sin.

Temporary Marriage

O ye who believe! Make not unlawful the good things which Allah hath made lawful for you, but commit no excess; for Allah loveth not those given in excess. (Surah al-Maʾidah 5:87)

We used to participate in the holy battles led by Allah's Apostle and we had nothing [no wives] with us. So we said, "Shall we get ourselves castrated?" He forbade us that and then allowed us to marry women with a temporary contract. (5.87 and hadith 7.62.130)

While we were in an army, Allah's Apostle came to us and

said, "You have been allowed to do the *Mut'a* [marriage], so do it." Salama bin al-Akwa' said: Allah's Apostle's said, "If a man and a woman agree [to marry temporarily], their marriage should last for three nights, and if they like to continue, they can do so; and if they want to separate, they can do so." I do not know whether that was only for us or for all the people in general. Abu Abdullah [*al-Bukhari*] said: "'Ali made it clear that the Prophet said, 'The *Mut'a* marriage has been cancelled [made unlawful].'" (hadith 7.62.52)

'Ali was told that Ibn 'Abbas did not see any harm in the *Mut'a* marriage. 'Ali said, "Allah's Apostle forbade the *Mut'a* marriage on the Day of the battle of Khaibar and he forbade the eating of donkey's meat." Some people said, "If one, by a tricky way, marries temporarily, his marriage is illegal." Others said, "The marriage is valid but its condition is illegal." (hadith 9.86.91)

Although a Qur'anic verse is used to show the permissiveness of a temporary marriage or *mut'a*, one must look to the *Hadith* to understand what a temporary marriage is and how it came into existence.

During the seventh century, when Islam was in its infant stage, men fighting holy war (jihad) under the leadership of Muhammed were often away from their families for extended periods. According to the *Hadith*, Muhammed allowed the men to marry women "temporarily" in order that they might have their sexual desires met (7.62.13). The justification for his declaration was Surah al-Ma'idah 5:87, "Make not unlawful the good things which Allah hath made lawful for you."

When a man and woman entered into a temporary marriage contract, the man agreed to pay the woman to stay with him for a designated period of time for the sole purpose of having sexual relations whenever he desired. The woman had no other responsibilities during this time. According to hadith 7.62.52, the marriage was to last a minimum of three nights.

From hadith 7.62.52 and 9.86.91, it appears that temporary

marriages were only permitted for a few years. Muhammed is said to have cancelled them.[30] Whether temporary marriages were cancelled or are still permitted is disputed among the different sects of Islam. The ShiᵖIte sect allows temporary marriages, but the Sunni sect does not.

THE DOCTRINE OF DIVORCE

Surah at-Talaq 65 offers twelve verses of advice and protection for women, including the teaching of a waiting period and provision for the wife who is divorced. Indeed, the traditional title for this chapter is literally "The Divorce." The process of divorce, which is both simple in its implementation and complex in its resolution, sheds much light on the disparity between the sexes.

Separation Before Divorce

And make not Allah's (name) an excuse in your oaths against doing good, or acting rightly, or making peace between persons; for Allah is One who heareth and knoweth all things. Allah will not call you to account for thoughtlessness in your oaths, but for the intention in your hearts, and He is Oft-Forgiving, Most Forbearing. For those who take an oath for abstention from their wives, a waiting for four months is ordained; if then they return, Allah is Oft-Forgiving, Most Merciful. But if their intention is firm for divorce, Allah heareth and knoweth all things. (Surah al-Baqarah 2:224–227)

Ibn ᶜUmar used to say about the Ila (which Allah defined in the Holy Book), "If the period of Ila expires, then the husband has either to retain his wife in a handsome manner or to divorce her as Allah has ordered." Ibn ᶜUmar added, "When the period of four months has expired, the husband should be put in prison so that he should divorce his wife, but the divorce does not occur unless the husband himself declares it. This has been mentioned by ʿUthman, ʿAli, Abu Ad-Darda, Aishah and twelve other companions of the Prophet." (hadith 7.63.213)

Although separation is not required, it appears that some men chose to separate from their wives before divorcing them. On the surface, one would assume that the husband chose separation in hope of reconciliation. But according to ʿAli, reconciliation was not always the husband's motive: "Sometimes, in a fit of anger or caprice, a husband would take an oath by Allah not to approach his wife. This deprived her of conjugal rights, but at the same time kept her tied to him indefinitely, so that she could not marry again. If the husband was remonstrated with, he would say that his oath by Allah bound him."[31]

The text seeks to suppress this custom, which was unfair to women, by limiting the period of separation to four months.

Obtaining a Divorce

A divorce is only permissible twice: after that, the parties should either hold together on equitable terms, or separate with kindness. (Surah al-Baqarah 2:229)

A man divorced his wife thrice (by expressing his decision to divorce her thrice), then she married another man who also divorced her. The Prophet was asked if she could legally marry the first husband (or not). The Prophet replied, "No, she cannot marry the first husband unless the second husband consummates his marriage with her, just as the first husband had done." (hadith 7.63.187)

The Prophet said, "Allah has forgiven my followers the evil thoughts that occur to their minds, as long as such thoughts are not put into action or uttered." And Qatada said, "If someone divorces his wife just in his mind, such an unuttered divorce has no effect. (hadith 7.63.194)

Whenever ʿAbdullah (bin ʿUmar) was asked about that, he
would say to the questioner, "If you divorced her thrice, she is
no longer lawful for you unless she marries another man (and
the other man divorces her in his turn)." Ibn ʿUmar further
said, "Would that you (people) only give one or two divorces,
because the Prophet has ordered me so." (hadith 7.63.249)

It is reported that Muhammed said, "Of all things permitted by
Law, divorce is the most hateful in the sight of Allah."[32] And yet, within
Islam, a husband can obtain a divorce, with unbelievable ease at any
time and for any reason. If a husband wishes to divorce his wife, he
simply says, "I divorce you. I divorce you. I divorce you." According to
hadith 7.63.194, "If a husband divorces his wife in a moment of anger,
the divorce is legal. A decree of divorcement, which is thought and
not uttered, is null."

Although the divorce is easily obtained, the *Qurʾan* limits the number of times that a husband can divorce his wife (Surah al-Baqarah
2:229). Commenting on 2:229, ʿAli suggests that the text was deemed
necessary because "where divorce for mutual incompatibility is allowed, there is danger that the parties might act hastily, then repent,
and again wish to separate. To prevent such capricious action repeat-
edly, a limit is prescribed. After that, the parties must definitely make
up their minds, either to dissolve the union permanently, or to live
honourable lives together in mutual love and forebearance."[33]

The Waiting Period

When ye divorce women, and they fulfil the term of their
(*ʿiddah*), either take them back on equitable terms or set them
free on equitable terms; but do not take them back to injure
them, (or) to take undue advantage. (Surah al-Baqarah 2:231)

O ye who believe! When ye marry believing women, and then
divorce them before ye have touched them, no period of *ʿiddah*
have ye to count in respect to them: so give them a present,

and set them free in a handsome manner. (Surah al-Ahzab 33:49)

O Prophet! When ye do divorce women, divorce them at their prescribed periods, and count (accurately) their prescribed periods: and fear Allah your Lord: and turn them not out of their houses, nor shall they (themselves) leave, except in case they are guilty of some open lewdness. (Surah at-Talaq 65:1)

Such of your women as have passed the age of monthly courses, for them the prescribed period, if ye have any doubts, is three months, and for those who have no courses (it is the same): for those who carry (life within their wombs), their period is until they deliver their burdens. (Surah at-Talaq 65:4)

Let the women live (in *'iddah*) in the same style as ye live, according to your means: annoy them not, so as to restrict them. And if they carry (life in their wombs), then spend (your substance) on them until they deliver their burden: and if they suckle your (offspring), give them their recompense: and take mutual counsel together, according to what is just and reasonable. And if ye find yourselves in difficulties, let another woman suckle (the child) on the (father's) behalf. (Surah at-Talaq 65:6)

If the period of Ila expires, then the husband has either to retain his wife in a handsome manner or to divorce her as Allah has ordered. (hadith 7.63.213)

When a husband divorces his wife, usually a waiting period or *'iddah* must occur. According to Surah at-Talaq 65:4, the waiting period is to last for three months unless the woman is with child. When a wife is pregnant, the waiting period is extended beyond the birth of the child to allow the mother to nurse the child (Surah at-Talaq 65:6). Surah al-Baqarah 2:233 allows the mother to nurse her child for at least two years. If a husband divorces his wife before he consummates the marriage, no waiting period is required (Surah al-Ahzab 33:49).

> Unless the wife has committed an immoral sexual act, the husband must allow her to live in his home during the waiting period (Surah at-Talaq 65:1). A differentiation in the lifestyle of a husband and his divorced wife is prohibited, and the husband is forbidden to annoy or restrict her so as to make her life miserable. (Surah at-Talaq 65:6)

> Upon the expiration of the waiting period, a husband must either take his wife back or let her go free. (Surah al-Baqarah 2:231 and hadith 7.63.213)

Remarriage

Should a husband desire to remarry his wife after he has *irrevocably* divorced her, he cannot do so immediately. First, the ex-wife must marry another man, and the marriage must be consummated. Then, if her new husband divorces her, she is permitted to remarry her former husband (hadith 7.63.187).

> If a husband divorces his wife (irrevocably), he cannot, after that, remarry her until after she has married another husband and he has divorced her. In that case there is no blame on either of them if they reunite, provided they feel that they can keep the limits ordained by Allah. Such are the limits ordained by Allah, which He makes plain to those who understand. (Surah al-Baqarah 2:230)

Surah al-Baqarah 2:229 allows a husband to divorce and remarry his wife twice. If a husband divorces his wife for a third time, the divorce is irrevocable.[34] According to ʿAli, the text is intended to discourage a husband who loves his wife from allowing "a sudden gust of temper or anger to induce him to take hasty action."[35]

TEACHINGS CONCERNING SEXUAL IMMORALITY

Muslims will often note that, even though their religion allows polygamy, they take a much stronger stance on sexual immorality than do most within the Christian community. As a matter of fact, they point to the lascivious nature of Western culture as proof of the supremacy of Islam over Christianity. Certainly the harsh nature of the punishments for those caught in sexual sin serves to deter many who would consider them, although the punishments are seen as violations of human rights in most nations.

Homosexuality

> If any of your women are guilty of lewdness, take the evidence of four (reliable) witnesses from amongst you against them; and if they testify, confine them to houses until death do claim them, or Allah ordain for them some (other) way. (Surah an-Nisa 4:15)

> If two men among you are guilty of lewdness, punish them both. If they repent and amend, leave them alone; for Allah is Oft-Returning, Most Merciful. (Surah an-Nisa 4:16)

According to 'Ali, "Most commentators understand [lewdness] to refer to adultery or fornication."[36] 'Ali, on the other hand, believes that lewdness "refers to unnatural crime between women, analogous to unnatural crime between men in 4:16."[37] One reason for his conclusion is that "no punishment is specified [in surah 4:15] for a man, as would be the case where a man was involved in the crime."[38]

The punishment for women proclaimed guilty of homosexual activity by four witnesses includes, but is not limited to, imprisonment for life. According to 'Ali, "We might presume, in the absence of a definite order ('some other way') that the punishment would be similar to that for men in the next verse."[39] Surah an-Nisa 4:16 appears to allow for exoneration, should the woman "repent and amend."

Adultery or Fornication

> The woman and the man guilty of adultery or fornication—
> flog each of them with a hundred stripes: let not compassion
> move you in their case, in a matter prescribed by Allah, if ye
> believe in Allah and the Last Day: and let a party of the Be-
> lievers witness their punishment. (Surah an-Naur 24:2)

> Let no man guilty of adultery or fornication marry any but a
> woman similarly guilty, or an Unbeliever: nor let any but such
> a man or an Unbeliever marry such a woman: to the Believers
> such a thing is forbidden. (Surah an-Naur 24:3)

> A man from the tribe of Bani Aslam came to the Prophet while
> he was in the mosque and said, "I have committed illegal sexual
> intercourse." The Prophet turned his face to the other side.
> The man turned towards the side towards which the Prophet
> had turned his face, and gave four witnesses against himself.
> On that the Prophet called him and said, "Are you insane?"
> (He added), "Are you married?" The man said, "Yes." On that
> the Prophet ordered him to be stoned to the death in the
> Musalla (a praying place). (hadith 7.63.195)

As can be seen by the text, sexual activity beyond the confines of
marriage is not to be taken lightly. The penalty for one who commits
adultery or fornication includes a physical aspect. The type of physical
punishment is often disputed. It is the opinion of some that the flogging spoken of in Surah an-Naur 24:2 is for those who commit fornication (unmarried persons), while those who commit adultery (married
persons) are to be stoned to death.[40] Hadith 7.63.195 appears to con-
firm the punishment of stoning for those who commit adultery.

The penalty for committing adultery or fornication also includes a
social dimension. According to Surah an-Naur 24:3, an individual
guilty of adultery or fornication is prohibited from marrying anyone
who is not also guilty of the same crime or an unbeliever.

THE DOCTRINE OF LIFE AFTER DEATH

How does eternity differ for men and women? Is the perceived disparity between men and women on earth continued in the afterlife? The experience of the life after the judgment, even in heaven, has qualitative differences for women. Though Christians will recognize the differences between the biblical description of eternity from Islamic paradise and hell, the emphasis on the variance between genders will be central.

A Fatalistic Salvation

> He forgiveth whom He pleaseth, and punisheth whom He pleaseth. (Surah al-Baqarah 2:284)

> So set thou thy face steadily and truly to the Faith: (establish) Allah's handiwork according to the pattern on which He has made mankind: no change (let there be) in the work (wrought) by Allah: that is the standard Religion: but most among mankind understand not. Turn ye back in repentance to Him, and fear Him. (Surah al-Rum 30:30–31)

> Allah's Apostle said, "Every child is born with a true faith of Islam (i.e. to worship none but Allah Alone) but his parents convert him to Judaism, Christianity or Magainism." (hadith 2.23.441)

> Allah's Apostle, the true and truly inspired, said, "(The matter of the Creation of) a human being. . . . Allah sends an angel who is ordered to write four things. He is ordered to write down his (i.e. the new creature's) deeds, his livelihood, his (date of) death, and whether he will be blessed or wretched (in religion). Then the soul is breathed into him. So, a man amongst you may do (good) deeds till there is only a cubit between him and Paradise and then what has been written

for him decides his behavior and he starts doing (evil) deeds characteristic of the people of the (Hell) Fire. And similarly a man amongst you may do (evil) deeds till there is only a cubit between him and the (Hell) Fire, and then what has been written for him decides his behavior, and he starts doing deeds characteristic of the people of Paradise." (hadith 4.54.430)

According to Muhammed, every child is a Muslim at birth, for he is "born with a true faith in Islam" (hadith 2.23.441). Commenting on Allah's handiwork in Surah al-Rum 30:30, 'Ali states, "As turned out from the creative hand of Allah, man is innocent, pure, true, free, inclined to right and virtue, and endued with true understanding about his own position in the Universe and about Allah's goodness, wisdom, and power."[41] It is the parents, according to Muhammed, who lead the children astray, converting them to other religions (hadith 2.23.441). Surah al-Rum 30:31 instructs the convert from Islam (*kafir*) to turn "back in repentance," which will result in the "restoration of [the] nature as Allah created it from the falsity introduced by the enticements of Evil."[42]

Although a woman is, supposedly, born with the inclination "to worship none but Allah" (hadith 2.23.441), she cannot have the assurance that Allah will forgive her if she repents. Surah al-Baqarah 2:284 reveals a capricious and fatalistic god who forgives only those whom he chooses to forgive. To make matters worse, the words of Muhammed, recorded in hadith 4.54.430, testify of a predetermined fatalism: "Allah sends an angel who is ordered to write four things. He is ordered to write down his (i.e. the new creature's) deeds, his livelihood, his (date of) death, and whether he will be blessed or wretched (in religion)."

Good Deeds of Believers Rewarded?

If any do deeds of righteousness—be they male or female—and have faith, they will enter Heaven, and not the least injustice will be done to them. (Surah an-Nisa 4:124)

Allah hath promised to Believers—men and women—Gardens under which rivers flow, to dwell therein, and beautiful mansions in Gardens of everlasting bliss. But the greatest bliss is the good pleasure of Allah: that is the supreme felicity. (Surah at-Taubah 9:72)

As to those who believe and work righteous deeds, they have, for their entertainment, the Gardens of Paradise. (Surah al-Kjahf 18:107)

Then those whose balance (of good deeds) is heavy—they will attain salvation: but those whose balance is light, will be those who have lost their souls; in Hell will they abide. (Surah al-Mu'minum 23:102–3)

And those who believe and work righteous deeds—them shall We admit to the company of the Righteous. (Surah al-'Ankabut 29:9)

He that works evil will not be requited but by the like thereof: and he that works a righteous deed—whether man or woman—and is a Believer—such will enter the Garden (of Bliss): therein will they have abundance without measure. (Surah Ghafir 40:40)

That He may admit the men and women who believe, to Gardens beneath which rivers flow, to dwell therein for aye, and remove their ills from them—and that is, in the sight of Allah, the highest achievement (for man). (Surah al-Fath 48:5)

There are many passages in the *Qur'an* that concur, as stated in Surah an-Nisa 4:124, that "if any do deeds of righteousness—be they male or female—and have faith, they will enter Heaven." There is, however, also a passage that appears to be contradictory. According to Surah al-Mu'minum 23:102–3, "Those whose balance (of good deeds) is heavy—they will attain salvation: but those whose balance is light, will be those who have lost their souls; in Hell will they abide."

Is a woman who is a believer promised Paradise, or does her fate "hang in the balance"?

Inhabitants of Paradise Will Feel No Sorrow

> They will be Companions of the Garden, therein to dwell (forever). And We shall remove from their hearts any lurking sense of injury—beneath them will be rivers flowing—and they shall say: "Praise be to Allah, who hath guided us to this (felicity): never could we have found guidance, had it not been for the guidance of Allah: indeed it was the truth, that the Messengers of our Lord brought unto us." And they shall hear the cry: "Behold! the Garden before you! Ye have been made its inheritors, for your deeds (of righteousness)." (Surah al-Aᶜraf 7:42–43)

According to Surah al-Aᶜraf 7:42–43, the inhabitants of paradise will not feel sorrow. ᶜAli explains that "a man who may have suffered or been disappointed may have a lurking sense of injury at the back of his mind, which may spoil his enjoyment on account of past memory intruding in the midst of felicity. In such cases memory itself is pain. . . . In the perfect felicity of the righteous, all such feelings will be blotted out."[43]

Inhabitants of Paradise Joined with Family

> Gardens of perpetual bliss: they shall enter there, as well as the righteous among their fathers, their spouses, and their offspring: and angels shall enter unto them from every gate (with the salutation): "Peace unto you for that ye persevered in patience! Now how excellent is the final Home!" (Surah ar-Raᶜd 13:23–24)

And grant, our Lord! that they enter the Gardens of Eternity, which Thou hast promised to them, and to the righteous among their fathers, their wives, and their posterity! For Thou art (He), the Exalted in Might, Full of Wisdom. (Surah Ghafir 40:8)

And those who believe and whose families follow them in Faith—to them shall We join their families: nor shall We deprive them (of the fruit) of aught of their works: (yet) is each individual in pledge for his deeds. (Surah at-Tur 52:21)

It appears from the various renderings found in the *Qur'an* that a righteous woman can look forward with great anticipation to a reunion with righteous family members in paradise. According to 'Ali, "Ancestors and descendants, husbands and wives, brothers and sisters, whose love was pure and sanctified, will find new bliss in the perfecting of their love and will see a new and mystic meaning in the old and ephemeral bonds."[44]

The Majority in Hell

The Prophet said: "I was shown the Hell-fire and that the majority of its dwellers were women who were ungrateful." It was asked, "Do they disbelieve in Allah?" (or, "Are they ungrateful to Allah?") He replied, "They are ungrateful to their husbands and are ungrateful for the favors and the good (charitable deeds) done to them. If you have always been good (benevolent) to one of them and then she sees something in you (not of her liking), she will say, 'I have never received any good from you." (hadith 1.2.28)

The Prophet said, "I looked at Paradise and found poor people forming the majority of its inhabitants; and I looked at Hell and saw that the majority of its inhabitants were women." (hadith 4.54.464)

The Prophet said, "I stood at the gate of Paradise and saw that the majority of the people who entered it were the poor, while the wealthy were stopped at the gate (for the accounts). But the companions of the Fire were ordered to be taken to the Fire. Then I stood at the gate of the Fire and saw that the majority of those who entered it were women." (hadith 7.62.124)

Although the *Qur'an* appears to be gender neutral when it presents the qualifications required of one to enter paradise, the *Hadith* appears to show a drastic gender imbalance among the inhabitants of hell. According to the *Hadith,* on three different occasions Muhammed had a vision of hell, in which he "saw that the majority of its inhabitants were women" (hadith 4.54.464).

NOTES

1. A. Yusuf ʿAli, *Holy Qurʾan: Text, Translation, and Commentary* (Brentwood, Md.: Amana, 1983), n. 47.
2. Ibid.
3. Ergun Mehmet Caner and Emir Fethi Caner, *Unveiling Islam* (Grand Rapids, Mich.: Kregel, 2002), 117.
4. ʿAli, *Holy Qurʾan*, n. 1966.
5. Ibid., n. 6004.
6. Ibid., n. 48.
7. Ibid., n. 6004.
8. Ibid., n. 996.
9. Ibid., n. 2103.
10. Ibid., n. 50.
11. Ibid., n. 776.
12. Ibid., n. 1006.
13. Ibid.
14. Ibid., n. 52.
15. Ibid., n. 1973.
16. Ibid., n. 1975.

17. Ibid., n. 49.
18. According to ʿAli, the expulsion also applied to Satan because "the Arabic plural is appropriate for any number greater than two" (Q note 53).
19. ʿAli, *Holy Qurʾan*, n. 55.
20. Ibid., n. 56.
21. Ibid., n. 255. Emphasis added.
22. Ibid., n. 516.
23. Ibid., n. 246.
24. Ibid., n. 700.
25. Ibid., n. 546.
26. Ibid.
27. Ibid., n. 547.
28. Ibid., n. 548.
29. Ibid., n. 639.
30. From the time of Muhammed's flight (or *hijra*) in 622, only ten years passed until his death in 632.
31. ʿAli, *Holy Qurʾan*, n. 253.
32. *Sunan Abu Dawud Hadith* 13.3.
33. ʿAli, *Holy Qurʾan*, n. 256.
34. Ibid., n. 260.
35. Ibid.
36. Ibid., n. 523.
37. Ibid.
38. Ibid.
39. Ibid., n. 525.
40. Ibid., n. 2954.
41. Ibid., n. 3541.
42. Ibid., n. 3543.
43. Ibid., n. 1021.
44. Ibid., n. 1837.

5

THE ESSENCE OF THE VEIL

The Veil as a Metaphor for Islamic Women

Susie Hawkins

In our generation, no single object has served as a derided symbol of Islamic oppression more than the veil. Indeed, many Westerners see the Islamic use of the veil as a sign of the medieval and misogynistic nature of Islam. Often, Christians forget that there have been similar teachings and practices in their own history. In this enlightening chapter, Susie Hawkins takes a different approach to the veil, viewing it as a metaphor for the plight of Islamic women and also as a commendable act of modesty that mirrors the desire for holiness by Muslim women. Hawkins travels the globe, speaking to thousands. Yet her style of speaking and writing reveals her secret—an intimate understanding of the hearts of the hurting. Read this chapter carefully for thoughts on the veil as an effective bridge of pre-evangelism.

Fatima is a fifty-three-year-old woman living in Damascus, Syria. Married, with six children, her day is busy with family responsibilities, grandchildren, household chores, and errands. But before she leaves the privacy of her home on any outing, she slips a baggy overcoat over her clothing, regardless of the temperature outside. Carefully covering her hair with a large scarf, she checks her reflection in the mirror, grabs her purse, and heads out the door.

Noor is a woman living in Tehran, Iran. Only twenty-eight years old, she already has four young children. She wishes she had the freedom that Fatima enjoys, however limited it may seem to others. Noor must veil herself in a *chador*, a large piece of fabric that covers her from head to toe, whenever she appears outside her home, which is rarely. Since the penalty in Iran for even a slight violation of Islamic dress is twelve months in prison and possible flogging, she avoids public places (as do most women).[1] Confined within the walls of her home, her only outings are occasional trips to the market and to the local mosque, where she joins the other women who are sequestered in separate quarters from the men.

However restrictive Noor's dress may be, it is preferable to that of her cousin Nadia, who married a strict Muslim from the United Arab Emirates (UAE) when she was only seventeen. According to UAE law, Nadia must wear an *abaya*, a full-length coat; the *burqa*, a face mask made of stiff fabric; and gloves that cover her arms to her elbows.

Then there is Leila, a twenty-five-year-old single woman living in her native city of San Diego, California. With a graduate degree from the University of California at Los Angeles (UCLA), Leila is the image of the successful, well-educated twenty-first-century woman, with a bright career ahead of her. Yet Leila, who was raised in a moderate Muslim home, has begun to cover her hair with a scarf and wear loose clothing in the traditional Muslim fashion when she appears in public. Having seriously reexamined her faith, she chooses to veil herself as a sign of her devotion to Islam.

Despite the vast diversity in their lives, all of these women "veil" themselves in obedience to the *Qur'an* and Islamic law. To some degree, most Muslim countries adhere to Islamic law, which requires women to cover their heads and often their entire bodies in public. Westerners may be surprised to learn that Muslims such as Leila, who live in secular countries where no veil is required, wear one anyway. These women do not see the headscarf as repressive or restrictive. Rather, it is viewed as a sign of their identity with Islam and their devotion to the Prophet Muhammed and his teachings.

THE MEANING OF THE VEIL

To understand Muslim women, we must grasp the importance and meaning of the veil and other pieces of traditional Islamic clothing. There is great diversity in the Islamic community worldwide, which is easily seen if you look at a map of the world. The Middle East and much of Africa consists of Muslim countries, and the largest Muslim population is in Southeast Asia. Europe and North America both have significant Muslim populations, including many converts. Although regional customs and traditions are influential in women's lives, many factors contribute to a remarkable unity among Muslim believers worldwide. The dictate of the *Qur'an* regarding veiling is one that almost all hold in common. The practice of veiling goes far beyond local mores, cultural perceptions of beauty, or even legal requirements.

The use of the veil has a long history in the East and was used by women years before the Islamic rise to power. Centuries before Muhammed, a veil signified that a women was in the king's harem. The isolation of wealthy upper-class women, signified by their veiling, was common in classical Greece, as well as in the Byzantine Empire, Persia, and India. Veiling became accepted among the followers of Muhammed primarily because it was a sign of wealth and position. The veil became accepted as the norm around the tenth century and has moved in and out of fashion since.[2]

The first followers of Muhammed wore traditional Arab dress. As time progressed and the *Qur'an* was applied to practical aspects of life, women began to cover their heads out of respect to the Prophet and his commands. It became an act of religious obedience. Now the veil is considered obligatory for most devout Muslim women. It is seen as a reflection of one's faith, purity, and adherence to Islam, an identification worn with honor.

With a few exceptions, most women in Muslim countries are required to wear some form of Islamic dress. In the West, Muslim women wear the veil usually by choice, although those who do so are viewed with suspicion or pity. Most American women are genuinely puzzled as to why any woman who lives in their neighborhood and works in their community would choose to wear an unnecessary headscarf or other head covering. To Western women, the scarf symbolizes repression and discrimination. To most Islamic women, it symbolizes devotion. Many have dared wear it even where it is outlawed, as in Turkey and Tunisia. The veil expresses their return to Islamic values. Understanding the deeper meaning of the practice of veiling should help us better understand and appreciate Muslim women who may be friends and neighbors. Rather than pity or fear a veiled woman, we should respect her in this choice and appreciate the long history that stands behind it.

Hijab in the Qur'an

Hijab is the general term used to describe the dress and veiling customs of Islamic women. *Hijab* comes from the Arabic word *hajaba*, which means "to hide from view."[3] The literal meaning of the word is "curtain." In its strictest sense, *hijab* refers to the scarf or veil worn over the head to cover the hair. In most Islamic countries, it is the minimum covering required for all women, including girls as young as nine years old. The *Qur'an* instructed Muhammed's followers on the proper way to address the Prophet's wives: "If you ask his wives for anything, speak to them from behind a curtain. This is purer for your hearts and their hearts" (surah 35:33).

This "curtain" was supposedly meant to be a protection against the sexual temptations that Muhammed believed would inevitably occur should men and women intermingle. He apparently believed that any contact between men and women would inevitably result in illicit sexual relations or at least lead to impure thoughts: "If a man and woman are alone in one place, the third person present is the devil," he said. This conviction is clearly seen in Islamic law and customs throughout the Muslim world.

Muhammed left similar instructions for female believers other than his wives:

> And say to the believing women that they should lower their gaze and guard their modesty, that they should not display

their beauty or ornaments except what they must ordinarily appear thereof; that they should draw their veils over their bosoms and not display their beauty except to their husbands, their fathers, their husbands' fathers, their sons, their husbands' sons, their brothers or their brothers' sons, or their sisters' sons, or their women, or the slaves whom their right hands possess, or male servants free of physical needs, or small children who have no sense of the shame of sex. (surah 24:31)

From this verse, the practice of veiling has evolved into the head and shoulder coverings and loose clothing that will not attract attention to a woman's body. The intent of veiling is to hide the woman's body and/or face to avoid attracting male attention. Because of this directive, devout Muslims consider veiling one of the Prophet's commands and a sign of a woman's adherence to the Qur'an: "Veiling has become a measure of a woman's honor, dignity, nationalism, and devotion to Islam."[4]

Just as Christians base their beliefs on Scripture, Muslims believe the Qur'an is the ultimate authority on life. Muslims believe that the Qur'an is to be studied in the original Arabic, which ensures the purity of the Prophet's words. There are no cultural modernizations or translations of the Qur'an, though the ulema (scholars) have provided translations with side-by-side Arabic text. Therefore the directives on veiling are taken literally rather than set in a historical context. Veiling is not considered a mode of dress of *past* cultures but an instruction for women in the past, present, and future.

Because the Qur'an is considered to be without error and cannot be criticized or defiled in any way, in some countries donning the *hijab* is considered the sixth pillar of Islam—especially in societies that observe *shari'a* law.

Shari'a Law

Understanding the authority of *shari'a* law gives a perspective from which to view the veiling and dress of Muslim women. All details of

life, including modes of dress, are addressed in one of three sources of
Islamic law: the *Qur'an;* the *Hadith;* and *shari'a* law. Of the three, *shari'a*
law is the most specific regarding women's dress. This code of law is
based on the *Qur'an,* the *Hadith,* and the work of Muslim scholars
throughout the early centuries of Islam. It is applied as a civil law code
to the most obscure areas of life. This volume of laws is best understood as a religious code for living, encompassing every aspect of life
from governmental law to personal dress codes to family life. Along
with *shari'a* descriptions of acceptable dress are the *fatwas,* legal opinions by Muslim scholars on interpreting a law in specific situations.
Religious Muslims believe that *shari'a* law describes the highest form
of Islamic life, as laid out in the *Qur'an* and *Hadith.* Though *shari'a*
law is expected to be part of the conscience of devout Muslims, often
it is also formally instituted as the legal code of Islamic states. Sometimes the law is strictly enforced, as in Saudi Arabia. In other countries it is more loosely interpreted, such as in the more open-minded
Malaysian society.[5] However it is enforced, *shari'a* governs all areas of
life, with severe penalties for disobedience.

Shari'a law is a concept foreign to most Westerners. Muhammed
saw little, if any, difference between the political and faith expressions
of Islamic belief. Where *shari'a* law is implemented, there is no separation of state and religion. The religious law is the civil law. H. A. R.
Gibb writes, "For the early Muslims there was little or no distinction
between 'legal' and 'religious.' In the *Qur'an* the two aspects are found
side by side, or rather interwoven one with the other, and so likewise
in the Hadith.... The meshing of law and religion results in the belief
that the law is divinely inspired and immutable."[6]

It logically follows that the belief that women should be covered
would be the law of the land. Contemporary veiling practices are a
response to interpretations of the *shari'a,* which gives women a specific set of garments referred to as "lawful dress."[7] The term "lawful
dress" is rather general and can be seen in the various styles of *hijab*
adhered to in Islamic cultures.

Under societies practicing strict adherence to *shari'a* law, women
can be shot for random violations, as shown in the video "Inside Af-

ghanistan: Behind the Veil," which was broadcast over the Cable News Network (CNN) during the 2002 war in Afghanistan. In this film, an undercover woman reporter secretly documented the plight of women under the oppressive Taliban. Covered with a thick veil and a small grille for her eyes, she found life impossibly difficult. Even if she accidentally showed her face or ankles, she could have been arrested.[8] This may be an extreme example, but similar practices are common in the most conservative Islamic countries, such as Iran and the Persian Gulf states. A woman who does not conform to the local standard of *hijab* is likely to be punished severely. Worse, she brings shame on her family in the eyes of her community in a culture where honor is tightly interwoven with the virtues of modesty and purity. The standards extend from dictates about wearing the *hijab* to laws regulating behavior toward men, however innocent it may be. Often a woman is forbidden even to look at a man other than her husband or an immediate family member.

"Honor depends on a woman remaining chaste; should she be violated in any way, the men of the family risk being seen as weak and perhaps even being ostracized."[9] Here is a crucial point in understanding the predicament of Muslim women. The reputation of their families rests on their shoulders. Even if a woman is completely innocent of any wrongdoing, she bears the shame when sexual misconduct occurs.

It is from this core idea that "honor killings" take place. In her book *Nine Parts of Desire*, author Geraldine Brooks tells of interviewing a young Palestinian woman who'd had a love affair with a young doctor. She became quite concerned for her life, fearing that she might become the victim of an "honor killing" by her father or younger brothers. Fortunately that did not happen, but when she attempted to protest this horrid practice with the help of Muslim women's rights advocates, she met with total resistance. According to Brooks, about forty Palestinian women a year are victims of this type of killing, which is believed to remove the shame of adultery from the family.[10] Most killings take place in rural villages, where the majority of residents are uneducated and live in poverty. One of the reasons that honor killings easily documented in this area is because, under Israeli occupation, murders are more likely to come to the attention of civilian police.[11] A number of Muslim women are speaking against this barbaric practice, such as Riffat Hassan, an activist who founded the International Network for the Rights of Female Victims of Violence in Pakistan. An Islamic theologian, she effectively speaks for women's rights, especially regarding honor killings. Hassan courageously appeared on the ABC news program *Nightline* in February 1999 to address this "misogynistic" practice.[12] Although the extreme application of *shariʾa* is not common in every Islamic country, it does occur.

> Certain aspects of the *sharia* law institutionalize women's oppression and have been a central concern of women's movements in the Arab world. The ability of men to divorce their wives without cause and with little penalty, the vesting of ultimate child custody with the father and his family, and the permitting of polygyny are all stipulations of the *sharia* still in force in most Arab countries.[13]

An example of this gender inequality is found in the law regarding rape in Pakistan. Women who are raped are charged with "adultery or fornication," known as *zinah*. To prove that there was truly a forced rape and not just consensual fornication, the victim must produce four honorable Muslim males who witnessed the actual act. Of course, this is impossible, so the perpetrator cannot be punished. The fault for the crime is charged to the victim, who has confessed to unlawful sexual relations just by alleging that a rape occurred.[14] For the woman, the suffering extends beyond the physical violation to the intense shame and reproach of society and her subsequent isolation due to the stain on her family name.

Prescribing *hijab* is the Islamic law's attempt to protect women from such troubles. Because sexual assaults are relatively common in Islamic societies, one can see why women might want to hide their faces and bodies to avoid male attention of any sort.

THE MANIFESTATIONS OF MODESTY

It is difficult to overstate the Islamic emphasis on female chastity, modesty, and social order to avoid sexual perversion. The virtue of veiling modesty shown in Qurʾanic verses about covering is of paramount importance. It is the basis for all *hijab*. However, the practical application of "modesty" can be subjective. Some interpret the *Qurʾan* to call for a simple head covering, as worn in Egypt, Morocco, and the more moderate Muslim countries. The *hijab* and the *jilba*, similar to a caftan, are a common ensemble there. On the other hand, the most extreme form of *hijab* was recently seen in Taliban-ruled Afghanistan, where women were required to wear the *burqa*, a shapeless form that covers the body from head to toe, with a type of face mask covering the eyes. These are also worn in regions of Pakistan.[15] One can only imagine the intense discomfort experienced during the summer heat. The *abaya,* a long black cloak with arm slits, is worn in the Persian Gulf countries. Iranian and some Lebanese women wear the *chador,* a large square fabric piece worn over the head and pinned under the chin. A *niqab*, worn in some regions, is a veil that covers the face and shoulders completely. In various parts of the Gulf states, women are even required to cover their hands with long gloves. Jordanian and Syrian women generally wear scarves and loose-fitting clothes, perhaps covered by a long coat. The fabric must be opaque except over the eyes where a type of netting is used. Despite the restrictions, it is interesting to note that there can be all sorts of fashion additions to the *hijab,* assuming a woman has the time and resources to decorate them. A visit to various Islamic Web sites for women shows all types of dress with varying colors, fabrics, trims, and designs. Debra Decker, a writer for the *Dallas Morning News*, tells of a journey she took to Saudi Arabia, Egypt, and Uzbekistan with the National Conference of Editorial Writers. Her assignment was to better understand Islam and its effect on women. She tells of interviewing Saudi women and observing, to her surprise, that when their *abayas* were removed in the privacy of a home, the women were dressed quite stylishly, with full makeup and Western haircuts.[16]

When the Taliban was vanquished in 2002, Afghan women offi-cially were freed from the suffocating burqas. However, most women continued to wear it, mystifying the Western reporters. Considering the importance placed on respect, virtue, and modesty, one can see why these women did not cast off their traditional dress. Their cul-ture demands that they maintain their covering and dress appropri-ately, despite the new legal freedom. Despite the law of the land, which may change from time to time, Muslim women must continue to bear the cultural and religious pressure to conform, even when dress is not regulated by law.

Application of *shariʾa* law in regard to *hijab* can be carried to ex-tremes in such countries as Saudi Arabia. Saudi women are seques-tered from the world by more than dress. They live very restricted lives. Whenever they travel outside the home, they must be accompa-nied by a male relative. They cannot drive.[17] In a restaurant, they may take their veils off to eat only if isolated in the privacy of family cu-bicles. Again we are reminded of the goal of *shariʾa* law to protect the culture from sexual immorality by separating woman in public, whether in dress or location. It is solely the woman's responsibility to avert any male attention or glances.

Strolling along the busy streets amid the traffic, shopping areas, and outdoor cafes of Morocco, one will rarely see a woman who is not a tourist sitting in a restaurant. Although Moroccan women are le-gally allowed to appear in a public place, cultural expectations do not give such freedom. There are so few women in public that even a vis-iting Western woman feels uncomfortable.

Modesty is protected by more than dress requirements. It is also safeguarded by a wide-ranging standard for behavior in social inter-action. Modesty as a virtue also applies to men, according to the *Qurʾan*. In public, a man is to be covered from the navel to the knee. In prac-tice, however, there is more inequity. Brooks tells of her experience on a Caspian Sea beach, where she saw Iranian men swimming in nor-mal swim trunks near women who were swimming in chadors.[18] Con-spicuously absent in *shariʾa* law are complementary constraints on the responsibility of men to guard their own thought or behavior.

SOCIAL AND POLITICAL IMPLICATIONS OF *Hijab*

Above, we pointed out the interesting phenomenon that Muslim women choose to wear the *hijab* in secular countries where it is not required. To the Western mind-set, the veil "symbolizes the relegation of women to a secluded world."[19] However, as part of a minority culture within a larger society, people often want to identify with their heritage, even if it means standing out and drawing discrimination. A sense of ethnic pride and identity may surface when one feels marginalized in a foreign culture. Many women feel that the veil frees them from sexual harassment and prejudice that can occur in work or social situations. After choosing to veil herself, one North American young woman wrote:

> No one knows whether my hair looks as if I just stepped out of a salon, whether or not I can pinch an inch, or even if I have unsightly stretch marks. Feeling that one has to meet the impossible male standards of beauty is tiring and often humiliating. . . . The idea is that modest dress and head coverings allow women to appear as individuals, rather than as purely physical objects.[20]

Islamic believers often claim that wearing the veil frees a woman from the tyranny of the beauty industry and its exploitation of the female body. Given that many women enjoy styling their hair, using makeup, and wearing fashionable clothing under their *hijab*, this is a questionable liberation. Nevertheless, the social message of the veil should not be overlooked. The trend to promote Islamic values in a secular culture is enforced by the wearing of *hijab*, and these women want respect for their beliefs.

Beyond culture, there are political implications to the veil. In 1923, Mustafa Kemal Atatürk began to secularize Turkey, moving the country away from Islamic law. One of his proclamations condemned the veil as "demeaning and a hindrance to a civilized nation."[21] This decree was not well received within the religious community.

In the 1930s, the shah of Iran outlawed wearing the hijab in an effort to Westernize society. His efforts to establish the Family Protection Acts of 1965 and 1975 improved the lives of Iranian women. However, in the Revolution of 1979, things quickly changed.[22] The laws were promptly overturned amid the backlash against the shah. Female protesters took to the streets, veiling themselves as a sign of the revolution. Their demonstrations protested the increasing Westernization of their society. As political pendulums swing away from modernization in Islamic societies, the veil becomes an outward sign of Islamic fidelity. In a political context, the veil symbolizes rejection of Western values, or the lack thereof, and support of Islamic law. It is a "shield against the invasions of Western-bred corruption and immorality."[23]

Among Islamic women's issues, the veil is an ongoing topic of controversy. Some groups, such as the Woman's Action Forum in Pakistan, argue that any dress code for women denies basic freedoms. Other groups that support stricter interpretations promote the dress codes, even publishing requirements for modest dress. Anyone who wishes to understand this debate can get a good introduction by touring Islamic Web sites that address the matter.

CONCLUSION

Reaching Muslim women with the liberating message of the gospel of Christ is indeed a challenge. However, understanding the important facets of their lives helps build a bridge of communication to friendship and opportunities for ministry. In regard to *hijab*, some observations might help us to do this.

First, recognize the virtue that lies behind veiling. "Modesty" is described in the *Oxford Dictionary* as "unpretentious, or not excessive." Surely, we Christian women can appreciate this value. We are exhorted to exhibit modesty in dress and behavior in 1 Peter 3. Because Western culture is characterized overseas by television programs that depict a low view of morality, Western Christians can see why Muslims sometimes come to consider Western society as the epitome of evil.

We can appreciate their serious approach to virtue and their willingness to adjust personal appearance to reflect genuine modesty.

Second, the veil is an obvious metaphor for the separation between genders required by Islamic law. Often emotionally and physically separated from their husbands and sons, as well as from the world around them, women can experience loneliness, depression, and frustration. Their profound responsibility for upholding the honor of the social order is visible to all—epitomized by the protective veil.

Despite the implications of the veil, there remains one undistorted truth: Islam regards the female body essentially as evil and the cause of sexual immorality. Geraldine Brooks, in reflecting on the deeper meaning of *hijab*, concluded that it is "the dangerous female body that somehow, in Muslim society, has been made to carry the heavy burden of male honor."[24]

In the Christian worldview, the body can be used as an instrument of sin, but the Bible teaches that we are "fearfully and wonderfully made" (Psalm 139:14 NIV). As we prayerfully consider how to reach Muslim women like Fatima, Noor, and Leila with the good news of Christ's love, we must remember that honor and dignity are important values to them. We also must remember that they may be hidden from human view by their covering, but they are not invisible to God. "Man looks at the outward appearance, but the LORD looks at the heart," according to 1 Samuel 16:7 (NIV). God knows each person's name, dreams, and fears. He loves to show His mercies and blessings. May God give us the grace and opportunities to speak His truth with unveiled love.

NOTES

1. Jan Goodwin, *Price of Honor* (New York: Penguin, 1995), 109.
2. Lyn Reese, "The Burqa, Chador, Veil and Hijab! Historical Perspectives on Islamic Dress; A Featured Essay from Women in the Muslim World," http://www.womeninworldhistory.com (9 September 2002).
3. Mary C. ʿAli, "The Question of Hijab: Suppression or Liberation?" Islamic School of Greater Kansas City, http://www.isgkc.com (24 October 2002).

4. Geneive Abdo, *No God But God* (New York: Oxford, 2000), 157.

5. Susie Steiner, "Sharia Law," http://www.guardianunlimited.com (3 September 2002).

6. H. A. R. Gibb, "The *Shariʾa*," http://www.answering-islam.org.uk.Books/Gill/sharia.htm (20 August 2002).

7. Abdo, *No God But God*.

8. "Inside Afghanistan: Behind the Veil" http://www.BBCNews.com (23 October 2002).

9. Reese, "The Burqa, Chador, Veil and Hijab!"

10. Geraldine Brooks, *Nine Parts of Desire* (New York: Anchor, 1995), 49.

11. Ibid., 50.

12. D. Cameron Lawrence, "People: Beyond the Burqa," http://www.louisville.com/loumag/loumagdisplay.html?article=8825 (20 October 2002).

13. Suha Sabbagh, ed., *Arab Women, Between Defiance and Restraint* (New York: Interlink, 1996), 11.

14. Goodwin, *Price of Honor*, 53.

15. Ibid., 56.

16. Debra Decker, "Behind the Veils," *Dallas Morning News*, 15 September 2002.

17. Ibid.

18. Brooks, *Nine Parts of Desire*, 3.

19. Reese, "The Burqa, Chador, Veil and Hijab!"

20. Monica Flores, "Hijab, the Muslim Woman's Head Covering," http://www.worldtrek.org/odyssey/africa/101399/101399mondjib.html (placed 13 October 1999).

21. Reese, "The Burqa, Chador, Veil and Hijab!"

22. Goodwin, *Price of Honor*, 112.

23. Abdo, *No God But God*, 158.

24. Brooks, *Nine Parts of Desire*, 32.

6

ISLAMIC PRACTICES IN THE REAL WORLD

Daily Life in Specific Islamic Countries

Mary Kate Smith

Mary Kate Smith is the pseudonym for a Christian missionary who serves in a region heavily populated by Muslim women. Her expertise in understanding the variant cultures and mores in Islam makes her writing invaluable. This chapter is specifically designed for those who want to interact with specific groups and cultures within the Islamic community without committing cultural offenses. Some of the fascinating details she provides have not been explained in any previous work. In various transitions, she includes missionary journal entries, which further enlighten the reader.

It is by grace you have been saved, through faith—and this not from yourselves, it is the gift of God—not by works, so that no one can boast. (Ephesians 2:8–9 NIV)

As a Christian missionary from the United States, I often wonder what my life would be like if I had been born to different parents or in another country. What would my favorite food be? Would my childhood have been as happy? Would I have gone to college? More than that, though, I wonder where I would be today if no one had shared the good news of Jesus' death and resurrection with me. I came out of my spiritual darkness twenty years ago because God was gracious to me. A few years later, God showed me that His gift of grace was not just for me but for all peoples. As a girl in vacation Bible school, I sang, "Untold millions are still untold," and gradually, that reality went from my head to my heart. He gave everything for me, so how could I withhold anything from Him? What if no one had ever told me?

Daily life for women in Islamic countries is a world separate from the experiences of most American women. Some Muslim women are beaten by their husbands, are virtual prisoners in their own homes, or in other ways are miserable, fearful victims of the culture and traditions that shape their lives. But some are trying to improve their lives and provide a better future for their daughters. Some are devout followers of Islam, submitting to the only religion they have ever known in an attempt to know their Creator. Understanding which culture a Muslim woman has come from can build bridges of genuine friendship and break down the barriers that separate them from the one true God.

Although the *Qur'an* and *Hadith* spell out many regulations and teachings about women's roles, rights, behavior, and societal expectations, how they are interpreted and carried out in daily life varies greatly from country to country, city to city, and even village to village. Traditions, ethnic background, and climate also play a part in shaping the life of Muslim women. Depending on her country or sect of Islam, a woman may spend her entire life confined to the home of her parents and then of her husband, or she may wear Western clothing, work in a shopping mall, and choose her mate in her own time. Among Muslim cultures, the disparity between personal freedom and religious legalism is significant.

Worldwide, there are an estimated 1.1 billion followers of Islam. Four countries are home to 48 percent of all Muslims: Indonesia, India, Pakistan, and Bangladesh.[1] This chapter will give miniature portraits of women's lives in those countries and in Afghanistan, Egypt, Iran, Saudi Arabia, Sudan, Turkey, and Uzbekistan. These nations represent a cross-section of North Africa, Central Asia, the Middle East, and South Asia. They also exemplify the diversity of Islamic beliefs and customs. Here we can only sample the various cultures as we examine the daily life and traditions of Muslim women. In some cases, we will be looking at only one part of a society—the rich, poor, urban, rural—or a dominant ethnic group. Even the three main sects of Islam—Sunni, Sufi, and Shi'a—interpret and carry out their religious practices in different ways. In some countries, religion has become so mixed with folk tradition that practices are followed in the name of Allah that have no basis in Islam whatsoever.

If this chapter encourages you to further study, please see the bibliography for some helpful resources.

Afghanistan (Sunni, Shi'a)

Population (2001): 22.7 million, 97.89 percent Muslim

More than twenty years of war have left many widows and fatherless daughters vulnerable and virtually invisible in Afghanistan. The Islamic Taliban rulers took away rights that had been granted to women by the previous government, such as education, health care, and employment. A lack of husbands or fathers to provide for or protect women, and no access to education or jobs, has led to high rates of suicide, depression, and destitution.[2]

Sitting at the crossroads of Asia and the Middle East, Afghanistan has more than seventy ethnic groups within its borders, each with its own version of Muslim life and culture. Only 15 percent of Afghan women are literate, and that number is declining.

In settled rural families, women are less restricted by *purdah*, or seclusion, so they are not strictly confined to their homes.[3] Some participate in harvesting and producing milk products. Some specialize in handicrafts like carpet or felt making. Nomadic women care for lambs, spin wool, and weave fabric from which their tents are made.

Women are largely viewed as the property of men. Daughters are valued for the dowry they will bring into the family when they marry.

With large families and generally low income levels, many girls are married at eleven or twelve years of age or as soon as they reach puberty. The Taliban has encouraged families to marry off their daughters as young as eight years old. Marriages are arranged by fathers of the bride and the groom, but the groom is usually in his mid-to-late twenties before he can support a wife. Men are also permitted more than one wife. A woman has the right to refuse marriage, but often she isn't told she's getting married until after all the arrangements have been made. To refuse then would bring shame to the family, something which is to be avoided at all costs.

Bangladesh (Sunni)

Population (2001): 129 million, 85.6 percent Muslim

People throughout Bangladesh wear loose, lightweight clothing because of the warm, humid climate. Most of the women wear *saris*, a long piece of plain or printed cloth wrapped around the waist and draped over one shoulder. A short blouse is worn underneath.

Purdah (seclusion) is practiced to varying degrees. Some women choose to veil themselves from head to toe when outside the home to protect the honor and respectability of their husband's family.

Marriages usually are arranged to strengthen social ties within the community. The woman's family must pay a bride price, sometimes over several years. If her family can't pay enough to satisfy the husband and his family, with whom she lives, the new bride may be mistreated by her in-laws, abandoned, or divorced. Poverty is widespread. The husband is expected to provide for the family, but many rely on the bride price to help support the entire family.

Women are known by their relationship to the men in their lives. They do not use their given names, but refer to each other as wives (*bou*) and mothers (*ma*), brother's wives (*chachee or mamee*) or mothers-in-law (*shashoree*). They are rarely viewed as individuals outside the world of men, be it their brother, son, father, or husband.[4] A Bangladeshi woman may consider it disrespectful to call her husband by his given name. Instead, he is referred to as "the father of" their son.

Bangladeshi men and women enjoy spending time visiting and chatting with relatives and friends. Men usually go to cafés, whereas women typically visit each other in their homes. In the home it is acceptable to sit crossed-legged on cushions or the sofa. A visitor may choose to bring a gift, but money must not be given, as it may cause offense. Bangladeshis use their right hand for eating. Avoid the "thumbs- up" gesture, which is considered rude.

Egypt (Sunni)

Population (2001): 68.47 million, 86.5 percent Muslim

The status of women has been changing in Egypt since the early 1970s. At times, rights concerning marriage, divorce, child custody, and alimony have been granted and then taken away. Today, shariʾa law is the official basis for government legislation.

For Egyptian men, divorce is easily obtained by saying "I divorce thee" on three separate occasions in the presence of witnesses. Practically, this leads to an increased desire for women to please their husbands and secure their position in the family. It has also increased the divorce rate. In the 1980s, about one in five marriages ended in divorce. A divorced woman is given some protection under the law. She usually retains all household furnishings, and any property and possessions she brought with her to the marriage. By law, the husband is also required to provide alimony for one year, or longer under special circumstances.

Marriage, arranged by the families of the couple, is usually based on the characteristics of the bride and groom. Physical attributes, education levels, temperament, and wealth are all considered when making a match. Most families will only arrange a marriage for the youngest daughter after all her older sisters are married. To be passed over is considered an indication that something is wrong with that daughter.

Estimates by relief organizations in Egypt indicate that 70–90 percent of women in Egypt have been circumcised. It is more a cultural tradition than a practice of Islam. Coptic Christians, who make up about 12 percent of the population, also follow this tradition.[5]

Some Egyptian women work outside the home. Professional positions are usually in the areas of education, engineering, and medicine. Half of all employed women hold low-paying jobs as street cleaners, janitors, hotel and domestic servants, and hospital aides.

When dining with Egyptian friends, it is an insult to clean your plate. This implies that the host didn't provide enough food. It's not unusual for dinner to be served as late as 10:30 p.m. Smoking is common among Egyptians.

India (Sunni, Shi'a)

Population (2001): 1.014 billion. 12.5 percent Muslim

Although predominantly Hindu, India has the second largest population of Muslims in the world, after Indonesia. About 90 percent of India's Muslims are Sunnis. The Ismailis are the largest Shi'a group.

The wedding parties of Indian Muslims include ceremonies held in different rooms for men and women in keeping with the tradition of segregation of the sexes. The husband is required to pay the wife at the time of the marriage.

Babies have their own rituals at birth. The call to prayer (Adhan) is whispered into the left ear and the profession of faith (Shahada) is whispered into the right ear. Honey or date paste is also placed in the mouth and a name is given. The baby has a first bath on the sixth day after birth.

Shrines in memory of great Sufi saints are important to Indian Muslims.[6] The tombs of the saints are seen as gateways to God. Because tales of miraculous events are sometimes associated with the shrines, pilgrims visit, hoping for relief from physical and personal problems. Many hang petitions on the walls surrounding the tombs, light incense, give money, and touch or kiss the tombs. There is at least one major Sufi shrine in every region of India.[7]

Hindu and Muslim women in India both practice purdah, but for different reasons. Both veil themselves outside the home in the presence of male strangers to protect family honor. Hindu women also cover themselves in the presence of their husband's family, including the women, as a sign of respect. Because women who practice *purdah* seldom leave home, most shopping is done by the men. If Muslim women go out at all, they wear a *burqa*, covering even the face.

Hot tea is a favorite beverage among Indians, and the main meal of the day usually is lunch. When invited to an Indian home, be prepared to leave your shoes at the door and be careful not to touch anyone with your feet. If this happens, an apology is expected. Whistling, especially in front of elders, should be avoided.

Indonesia (Sunni, Shi'a)

Population (2001): 213 million, 80.3 percent Muslim

Islam was introduced into Indonesia through a complex history of interrelationships, but the more mystical Sufi bent most likely came through Indian traders. It was absorbed easily into local customs, and now includes orthodox Islam as well as blends of Islamic, Hindu-Buddhist and animistic beliefs called *kebatinan*. Kebatinan is considered a pantheistic religion, because it encourages ancestral spirit worship and sacrifices to appease angry deities.[8]

Women began to gain freedoms in Indonesia in 1967 under the rule of President Suharto. He had only one wife and during his tenure a new law made polygamy illegal for male civil servants and the military. The traditional roles of women mentioned in the country's constitution as the "five duties of women" are wife, mother, household manager, worker (to contribute to the family income), and member of women's social organizations whose aim is to improve society.

Women wear *sarongs*, a full-length wraparound skirt, with a *kebaya*, a tight, low-cut, long-sleeved blouse. Some also wear a *seledang*, a long cloth draped over the shoulder, which is sometimes used to carry babies or objects. Veiling is optional.

Visitors to an Indonesian home commonly give a small gift.

Usually, tea or coffee will be served, but it should not be drunk until the host invites you to do so. If an unexpected visit is made during a meal, it is polite to invite the guest to eat with you. Indonesian food is usually very spicy. When receiving a gift or eating, using the left hand is considered offensive, as is touching the head (which is the most sacred part of the body) or showing others the bottoms of your feet or shoes.

Iran (Sunni, Shi'a)

Population (2001): 67.7 million, 99 percent Muslim

Seventy-five distinct ethnic groups are at home in Iran.[9] These include nomads, farmers, wealthy, poor, educated, fishermen, blue- and white-collar workers, Islamic fundamentalists, and nominal or cultural Muslims. Before the Islamic revolution in 1979, the Iranian government, under the leadership of Shah Mohammad Reza Pahlavi, sought modernization and secularization, and established laws guaranteeing basic rights to women. As the Islamic Republic established itself in the early 1980s, women's rights eroded in the name of Islam. Public spaces became segregated. The legal age of marriage was lowered to thirteen for women and fifteen for men. Women could no longer work in certain professional arenas, including being a judge.[10]

Many highly educated Iranians now live outside of Iran because they disagreed with the revolutionary government. Some minority groups such as Christians, Jews, and Baha'is left to escape persecution and the threat of death.

Shi'a Islam is the main sect of Islam followed in Iran. Unlike Sunni Islam, it recognizes mut'a, or temporary marriage. According to Iranian Shia scholars, mut'a is a contract in which a man and woman agree to become man and wife for a specified time. The contract can be in force for several hours or for as long as ninety-nine years. The man agrees to pay the woman, but she has no inheritance or rights as a wife once the agreed upon time expires. If children are produced, the man must support them. Mut'a was permitted by Muhammed early in Islam during the Victory of Mecca when Muslims did not have stability and faced difficulties from the pagans around them. It was later made unlawful, according to Sunni interpretation.[11]

Extended family ties are extremely important in Iranian culture. Members of an influential family are strategically distributed throughout society and are prepared to help each other to keep up the family status. As a guest in an Iranian home, it is important to give compliments carefully. Saying, "That painting looks very nice on your wall," rather than, "That's a nice painting," will ensure that it stays there. A host would rather give you the object you compliment than cause you to covet and risk ruining your friendship.

Pakistan (Sunni, Shi'a)

Population (2001): 156.5 million, 96.08 percent Muslim

A *shalwar-qamiz* is the garment of choice for both men and women in Pakistan. It consists of baggy trousers covered by a knee-length, loosely fitting long-sleeved shirt. A woman's *shalwar-qamiz* is often colorful and may be decorated with embroidery. In urban areas such as the capital, Islamabad, a woman may go out in public with a light scarf over her hair, but in some provinces, women rarely venture out of their homes. When they do, they wear a *burqa* or a *chador*, a loosely draped cotton cloth used to cover the head and body. A Pakistani bride traditionally wears a red wedding dress for her arranged marriage.

In one instance, an unchaperoned Western woman was walking down the street covered in a *chador*. Only her face and shoes were visible. A man reached out and touched her as she walked by. As her local female friends had coached her, she took off her shoe and hit the man with it, saying, "Don't you have a mother?" She was shaming him for dishonoring his family by not observing *purdah* and distancing himself from a woman who was unknown to him.

He responded, "Yes, I have a mother, but I don't have a wife."

Family honor is protected at all costs, and a woman's behavior is at the center. For this reason, society limits a woman's mobility, often restricting her to her home and courtyard, thus ensuring she will not come into contact with the opposite sex and possibly bring shame to the family. If a woman's honor is under suspicion, she may become a victim of the tribal tradition of *karo kari*, or honor killing. Although contrary to Islam, in 1999 five hundred people were killed in the name of honor. Their murderers were not held accountable. According to *karo kari* tradition, men can be killed, but the majority of deaths are among women, most often at the hands of their father, brothers, or husband. The practice also goes on in Jordan and in Muslim communities in Israel.[12]

By 1990, women made up 13 percent of the official labor force. Few willingly admit that women contribute to the financial support of their family, but especially among the rural poor the contribution of women is significant. Often they work as midwives, nannies, and in agriculture, planting rice and raising chickens. Poverty is high among the more than 160 ethnic groups, including many refugees from Afghanistan.

Pakistani cuisine includes baked and deep fried breads, such as *chapattis* and *nan;* peas, rice, lentils, and meat curries. Strong, hot tea with milk is served, usually by the oldest female in the home. Mutual hospitality and courtesy are of great importance at all levels, whatever the social standing of the host.

Saudi Arabia (Sunni, Shi'a)

Population (2001): 21.6 million, 92.83 percent Muslim

As protector of the birthplace of the religion, Saudi Arabia is considered the guardian of true Islam. Millions of Muslims worldwide fulfill one of the five pillars by making the *hajj* (pilgrimage) to Mecca. Non-Muslims are forbidden to visit the holy cities of Mecca and Medina. Public displays of non-Islamic belief, such as wearing a cross or carrying a Bible, are illegal, and Christians who do so are shunned.

Women, whether Saudi or expatriates living in the country, face discrimination in nearly all areas of life. They are not allowed to drive, need written permission from male relatives to travel, and cannot marry non-Muslims. A woman's testimony in court is given half the weight of the testimony of a man. Women must cover themselves from head to toe in public with an *abaya*, a full-length black cloak, and those who do not risk beatings or detention by the *Mutawwa'in*, the religious police of the Committee for the Propagation of Virtue and the Prevention of Vice, which enforces Islamic norms by monitoring public behavior.[13] Women are not permitted to mingle with men who are not members of their family.

Many upper- and middle-class Saudis have been educated in the United States or Europe and speak English fluently. Many go abroad as tourists or on business, which may be their only exposure to the gospel. Missionaries and anything Christian, such as the *Jesus* film, Bibles, and other religious literature, are illegal in Saudi Arabia.

Five times a day, the call to prayer rings out from mosques everywhere. All businesses close for half an hour. The normal workweek is Saturday through Wednesday. Friday is the Muslim holy day, as well as the public execution day. Drug trafficking and some other offenses are punishable by beheading. Women usually are executed by firing squad in a private location. In recent years, between twenty-five and ninety people have been executed each year.

Saudi food includes pita bread with every dish. The main meal, lunch, typically includes kebabs of chicken or lamb, vegetables, and soup. Pork is forbidden under Islamic law, as are alcoholic beverages. When inviting a Saudi friend to share a meal, expect to be turned down at least once.

Sudan (Sunni)

Population (2001): 29.5 million, 65 percent Muslim

Civil war in Sudan divides the Islamic north from the predominantly Christian south. Islamic radicals have instituted *shari'a* law over the entire country and have used brutal tactics to gain control of the south and its oil reserves. Every Sudanese refugee woman has been affected in some way by violence. Her village may have been destroyed, loved ones murdered, or perhaps she, or someone she loves, has been imprisoned, beaten, or raped.[14]

Female circumcision is widely practiced in Islamic northern Sudan. It is a cultural tradition that is neither commanded nor forbidden in the Qur᾽an.[15] It is often performed on young girls without anesthesia in unsanitary conditions and may lead to health problems, such as increased risks during childbirth and possibly death. Female midwives perform the operation, which is seen as a normal protection of a young girl's virginity and the family's honor by repressing her sexual desire before puberty. It is estimated that as many as 2 million women worldwide have been circumcised.[16]

The Zar cult has had an enormous impact upon the private and social relationships of Sudanese women. Zar is a ceremony conducted only by women practitioners to pacify evil spirits and to cleanse women of afflictions caused by demons or *jinn*. Illnesses, including depression, infertility, and psychological disorders, are attributed to possession by hostile spirits. A Zar ceremony not only frees the one possessed but is a great social occasion for women.

Turkey (Sunni)

Population (2001): 66.6 million, 99.64 percent Muslim

In 1926, Mustafa Kemal Atatürk founded the secularized Republic of Turkey, and Atatürk is still revered by many Turks. Many prominently display photographs of him in their homes and businesses. When the secular republic was formed, women gained rights unavailable under the laws of the previous Islamic state. The veil and polygamy were abolished. Women were allowed to receive equal inheritance with male relatives, as opposed to receiving half, as under Islamic law. Their testimony in a court of law became equal to that of a man. As the republic grew, women also gained the right to vote and to receive equal wages.

However, this secular republican form of government was shaken by the election of late 2002, when the Islamic *shari᾽a* party won in sweeping fashion. As this is written, the fate of Atatürk's revolutionary changes is unknown. Perhaps the country will slip back toward Islamic theocracy.

Meanwhile, it is not uncommon in larger cities, such as Istanbul, to see two women walking arm in arm, one veiled in black from head to toe and the other wearing a miniskirt and a top that reveals her midriff. Other women prefer a style of clothing that falls between secular attire and full-body veiling, wearing long coats and color-coordinated headscarfs in public. Regardless of their everyday clothing, all women cover up when attending a mosque or reciting prayers.

Aysha and her sisters ran a small flower shop in Istanbul. After several months of visits, I noticed that Aysha sometimes would disappear to a back room for about thirty minutes. Her sister told me she was doing *Namaz*, meaning prayers. Once, she came out for a moment, and I noticed she had exchanged her miniskirt for a much longer, loose-fitting skirt and was wearing an embroidered scarf that fully covered her hair. When the prayers were over, she reappeared in her miniskirt and bundle of curls piled fashionably on top of her head. She turned the radio back on and sang along with the latest imported American pop music with no idea of what the lyrics meant.

Although many women have joined the workforce, the role of wife and mother is still a priority. When a child is born, relatives bring gifts of gold to the mother and numerous presents for the baby during the first three days. After that, neighbors and friends may visit, also bringing gifts.[17] Living with extended family is quite common in rural areas, and a woman becomes part of her husband's family when she marries.

When visiting a Turkish friend, street shoes are exchanged for house shoes or slippers when entering the home. Turkish people are generally very hospitable to foreigners. Traditional Turkish coffee is very strong, and many Turks prefer to drink strong tea with sugar, usually served boiling hot in small glasses. Turkish food is usually quite tasty to the Western palate, but does include some unusual foods such as *ayran*, a salted yogurt drink, and *kokorech*, a spicy sandwich filling made of intestines grilled on a spit.

Uzbekistan (Sunni)

Population (2000): 24.3 million, 83.5 percent Muslim

In Uzbek culture, a woman's role as wife and mother and her contribution to family life are highly valued. Because of this, even many educated women put aside career ambitions to get married and raise a family. Marriage sometimes begins as young as age sixteen, though twenty to twenty-four years old is the average. Arranged marriages are still practiced, especially in rural areas.

I was walking on air when I entered the living room of our apartment. My American roommate was having tea with two of her Uzbek friends.

"Mary Kate is getting married, too," my roommate told one of the girls who was getting married in about a month. "Show them your ring."

I held out my left hand and smiled blissfully. My reaction to their first question was a pitiful display, and I'm sure my jaw hit the floor.

"Do you like him?" she asked.

"Like who?"

"Your fiancé? You've met him. Is he nice?"

"Of course I've met him. I'm going to marry him, aren't I?"

What for me held pure joy and excitement was for this Uzbek woman a scary unknown. Hers was an arranged marriage to a man she had never met from her village.

When Uzbekistan first became a state of the former USSR, Muslim women gained many rights under the communist government. After its independence, the Republic of Uzbekistan slowly revived Islamic traditions. In the cities, women may still wear modern, though conservative, clothes. In rural areas, many women have chosen or been coerced by family members and neighbors to wear headscarfs or veils.[18] Dresses made from a traditional multicolored silk fabric called *atlas* are also very popular.

As a guest in an Uzbek home, one can expect to be overwhelmed by the hospitality offered. Guests are usually given the seats farthest from the door. Traditionally, a half-full cup of tea is an invitation to stay and enjoy as much food and conversation as possible. A full cup indicates that it is time to leave. A host will also offer food at least three times before believing a guest has had enough to eat. Placing one's right hand over one's heart indicates an extra degree of sincerity and thanks for hospitality or any other act of kindness and friendship.

BARRIERS AND BRIDGES

Recognizing cultural barriers will ease frustrations and possibly prevent misunderstandings. American culture, "Christian" traditions, and even history have created walls of bitterness, hatred, and division, sometimes lasting centuries. The Crusades, sanctioned by the Roman Church in the Middle Ages, were fought in Jesus' name. The United States is generally considered a Christian country, yet its citizens are perceived to have little or no moral standards. Imported U.S. television entertainment programs like *Friends* or *Baywatch* are the only glimpses of American life that people overseas see. A sincere follower of Jesus can turn those barriers into bridges for the gospel to enter a culture or a person's life.

For one Christian family in Afghanistan, the walls of *purdah* seemed impossible to overcome, until the whole family was invited into an Afghan home for a meal. According to custom, the husband was shown into a room reserved for the men of the family. As a man, he could not be allowed access to the host's wife, even for a moment. His wife and children were shown into the "family" room, to spend the evening with the hostess and her children. While the men hotly debated their religious differences and the problems with Christianity during their meal, the women guests shared stories of life in America and how being a follower of Jesus had changed their lives. The men of the host's family came into the family room from time to time during the evening. The amazing thing was that they listened to the Christian woman without interrupting. Because women are considered inferior to men, they would not debate religion with her. The Holy Spirit used her words to penetrate the hearts of the men while her husband's words seemed to fall on deaf ears.

Purdah can be a barrier, because it limits or denies access of women to one another. However, it also can be a bridge to Christ. Women cover themselves with a veil and remain at home to protect themselves and others from sin, shame, and death (honor killings). Christ's blood covers us and protects us from spiritual death, the ultimate consequence of our sin. Though we may not like or agree with the cultural practices of our Muslim friends, we must learn to recognize the potential bridges their traditions may create. As Westerners, our knowledge of other cultures must grow. Learning that your new Afghan friend is really from the Baluch people group will surprise her, show that you care, and probably deepen your friendship.

More women from Muslim countries are coming to the West each year. They need friends who will go out of their way to show them the ropes of the local culture and daily life. They need help with everything from grocery shopping to understanding holidays and traditions. They need recommendations for sources of good medical care, a decent hair styling, and child care. They face the challenges of understanding the directions for using a dishwasher and translating notes from their children's teachers. They also need friends who will give them the true hope found in Christ when the American dream turns to disappointment. The reality is that life for women in the West *is* generally better than in other parts of the world, but only heaven is perfect.

NOTES

1. "The Muslim World: Information and statistics about the Muslim population of the world," http://islam.about.com/library/weekly/aa120298.htm (1 November 2002).

2. Patrick Johnstone and Jason Mandryk, *Operation World Prayer Calendar* (Toronto, Ontario: Gabriel Resources, 2001), 1–3.

3. Susan P. Arnett, "Purdah," http://www.kings.edu/womens_history/purdah.html (1 November 2002). *Purdah* is the practice that includes the seclusion of women from public observation by mandating the wearing of concealing clothing from head to toe and by the use of high walls, curtains, and screens erected within the home. *Purdah* is practiced by

Muslims and by various Hindus, especially in India. The limits imposed by this practice vary according to different countries and class levels. Generally, those women in the upper and middle class are more likely to practice all aspects of *purdah* because they can afford not to work outside the home.

4. Jennifer Morris, "The Changing Face of Women in Bangladesh," http://columbia.edu/cu/sipa/PUBS/SLANT/SPRING97/morris.html (27 October 2002).

5. Deborah Horan, "Egypt-Women: The Miserable Tradition of Female Circumcision," http://www.oneworld.org/ips2/sep/circum.html (28 October 2002).

6. "Islam and Muslims: Sufi Islam," http://atheism.about.com/library/FAQs/islam/blfaq_islam_sufi.htm (1 November 2002). The original Sufis were mystics who followed a pious form of Islam and who believed that a direct, personal experience of God could be achieved through meditation and self-discipline. Over time, Sufism became institutionalized, and individual mystics attracted groups of students and followers who learned to follow the mystic's path, or *tariqa*. The *tariqa* is a set of mental and sometimes physical exercises designed to aid in the development of communion with God.

7. "India: Origins and Tenets," http://lcweb2.loc.gov/cgi-bin/query/r?frd/cstdy:@field(DOCID+in0059) (13 October 2002).

8. "Indonesia: Islam," http://lcweb2.loc.gov/cgi-bin/query/r?frd/cstdy:@field(DOCID+id0052) (13 October 2002).

9. "Prayer Profile: The Astiani of Iran," http://www.bethany.com/profiles/p_code5/909.html (1 November 2002).

10. Shiva Balaghi, "Women in Iran: An Historical Review;" http://www.pbs.org/visavis/women_mstr.html (29 October 2002).

11. Osama Abdallah, "Temporary Marriage (Muta) . . . ," http://answering-christianity.com/temporary_marriage.htm (29 September 2002).

12. Fariha Razak Haroon, "Annihilation of Women Goes On," http://inrfvvp.org/documents/annihilation.htm (29 October 2002).

13. "Saudi Arabia: Human Rights Developments," http://www.hrw.org/wr2k/Mena-08.htm (29 October 2002).

14. Julia Aker Duany, "Believers Together with Glad and Sincere Hearts:

Special Needs of Sudanese Girls," http://southsudanfriends.org/specialneeds.html (27 October 2002).

15. David L. Gollaher, *Circumcision: A History of the World's Most Controversial Surgery* (New York: Basic Books, 2000), 192.

16. Ibid., 189.

17. "Anatolian Culture Part 3: People," http://turkishodyssey.com/turkey/culture/people.htm (26 October 2002).

18. Mahbuba Ergesheva, "Challenges of Women in Changing Uzbekistan," http://women.freenet.uz/proj/1_1.html (26 October 2002).

7

CHERISHED COMMODITY

Daughters in Islam

Suzanne Lea Eppling

The plight of daughters in Islam has been enumerated in secular literature, where one can read about female circumcision and even infanticide of female babies. Suzanne Lea Eppling takes a fresh approach by injecting Christian empathy into the equation. One cannot bemoan a tragedy without offering some solution to the problems that contributed to the crisis. Eppling does that with exacting expertise. Her treatment of the subject is often graphic. As a pastor's wife and mother of a young daughter, she offers profound insight into the often catastrophic ordeals that face Muslim girls.

A reporter sat with an Afghani farmer and his wife, discussing life in post-Taliban Afghanistan. The farmer talked to the reporter about life with his three children. His wife added, "Yes, we have three boys, but we also have four girls."[1] In the accounting of his family, this Afghan farmer did not consider his daughters worthy of mention. Why wouldn't this father also take pride in having daughters? Why is a male child of more value than a female child?

The answer extends back to pre-Islamic Arabian attitudes. Daughters were raised as showpieces. During times of war and poverty they were not as useful as boys, and were, therefore, expendable. Female infants were often laid facedown in the desert sand or buried in a waiting grave as soon as they were born.

One reason for female infanticide in ancient Arabia was to avoid disgrace if an enemy captured a daughter. The story is told about the daughter of a leader of Tamim who married the son of her captor and refused to leave when her father came with the ransom. The father's pride was so offended that he killed his remaining daughters by burying them alive and never allowed another daughter to live. Other chiefs followed his example, fearing their daughters might cause them shame.[2]

With the birth of Islam in the Arab world and the writing of the *Qur'an,* Muhammed banned the practice of female infanticide: "Hence, do not kill your children for fear of poverty: it is we who shall provide sustenance for them as well as for you. Verily, killing them is a great sin" (surah 17:31). "When news is brought to one of them, of [the birth of] a female [child], his face darkens, and he is filled with inward grief! With shame does he hide himself from his people, because of the bad news he has had! Shall he retain it on [sufferance and] contempt, or bury it in the dust? Ah! What an evil [choice] they decide on?" (surah 16:58–59). Other texts prohibiting female infanticide are surah 6:137, 140, and 151; 60:12; and 81:8–9.

Even though the *Qur'an* addresses the added value to women, the treatment of girls as inferior beings persisted and continues in many Muslim societies today. Hadithic literature indicates that Muhammed called for equal treatment among children and asked Muslims to live with daughters and sisters in "a good manner." With so much left to individual interpretation of what living in a "good manner" would be, some argue that although Muhammed banned the murder of female babies, he really did not grant them more than the mere right to live.[3]

Another factor that contributes to valuing a son more than a daughter is the clear teaching in the *Qur'an* that females are genetically inferior to males. The diminished mental capacity of females stems from the Muslim belief that Allah created men and women with individual purposes, and equipped each physically and mentally for the tasks given.[4] Allah created women to bear children and care for them (surah 2:233; 7:189.) Therefore, Allah did not need to give them the ability to do more than understand how to nurture children and be keepers at home. Muslims believe that men were created to provide for and protect the female members of the family, leaving women free to fulfill their roles as wife and mother (surah 2:233, 240; 4:34.)

The Bible also assigns different roles to the respective genders, with a decided difference: Men and women are different in function yet equal in essence before God. The equality in essence in the eyes of God is the reason there is such an enormous gap between the two belief systems regarding women. For Christian parents, the Bible is the basis for how to treat children and what to teach them. My seven-year-old daughter learns from the pages of the Bible that she has been created in the image of God and that He has a unique plan for her life. If she chooses to marry, then God will expect her to be the godly wife described in Titus 2:3–5: "The older women likewise, that they be reverent in behavior, not slanderers, not given to much wine, teachers of good things—that they admonish the young women to love their husbands, to love their children, to be discreet, chaste, homemakers, good, obedient to their own husbands, that the word of God may not be blasphemed" (NKJV).

These instructions leave room for each Christian woman to find fulfillment in whatever areas God leads her to pursue. My daughter currently has three long-term goals for life: (1) become a veterinarian; (2) play tennis on television; and (3) marry the blond little boy from church. As she seeks to follow God with all of her heart, life might come to include any or all of those things. Her life is not defined by what role she fills, but by how she lives as a follower of Jesus Christ and what kind of person she becomes in His hands.

EDUCATION

Muslims believe that Allah has not given women the same mental capacity as men to work because their assigned roles as wives and mothers do not require it. Understanding this explains why so many Muslim girls are not encouraged to pursue an education. The male dominance of the educational system safeguards the culture from female inferiority.

Little by little, women in Muslim countries are gaining access to public education. The level of education available to a Muslim girl largely depends on her country of birth, and whether she is brought up in a rural or urban setting, as well as the mind-set of her father and the other male members of the family. A girl who is allowed to go to school faces many restrictions. The policy for female education as defined by Saudi Arabia is "to bring her up in a sound Islamic way so that she can fulfill her role in life as a successful housewife, ideal wife, and good mother, and to prepare her for other activities that suit her nature such as teaching, nursing, and medicine."[5]

Women are limited in their education in many Muslim countries because they can work in one of only a few select fields due to gender segregation laws. Teaching is seen as a natural extension of a woman's nurturing role with children. Medicine is the single field where it is generally accepted for men and women to work side-by-side.

Muslim education is more religious than secular in nature. Traditionally, children were tutored at home in the teachings of the *Qur'an*. The foremost goal was to help them become devout Muslims. There were no publicly funded schools in Saudi Arabia until 1951, when secondary schools opened for boys. Many Muslims view a secular education as a waste of time for girls, due to their high calling of birthing children.

By 1960, public funding was available for separate girls' schools, but only 2 percent of the girls in Saudi Arabia were enrolled. The female literacy rate had been as low as 2 percent in 1970. By the late 1980s and early 1990s, 44 percent of women were enrolled in school, and literacy among Saudi women had grown to 48 percent. The numbers in Saudi Arabia are even more revealing, considering that there are more than 10 million women there, and half are estimated to be under the age of twenty.[6] It is interesting to note that physical education is taught only to the boys in Saudi schools, and home economics is taught only in the girls' institutions.

The literacy rate among Muslim females must be a consideration in how to introduce them to the love of Christ. Many cannot read a gospel tract or a copy of the Bible. They live in spiritual darkness. For example, a national Family Health Survey cited the illiteracy rate among Haryana women (Muslims in India) at 98 percent.

All people have the right to reject Christ and follow the religion of their choice, but it should at least be their choice. The restriction from reading denies many Muslim women the freedom to discover the truth regarding Jesus. The only way that an illiterate Muslim woman will ever hear that Jesus offers a transformed life is through the oral testimony of a Christian woman.

If a young woman has received basic schooling, several roadblocks stand between her and higher education. Because colleges and universities in Saudi Arabia are segregated, a young woman is relegated to watching her class by closed circuit television and communicating with the male professor without seeing him or being seen by him. Segregation also prohibits her from browsing in the library, forcing the young woman to write down specific titles and sending for the books. There are colleges for women, but very few of them have libraries.[7] Despite these cultural obstacles, woman in Saudi Arabia continue to struggle for higher education. By 1989, there were as many women in Saudi colleges and universities as there were men, marking a 132 percent increase in one decade in the number of women in higher education.

Female education, along with many other rights for women, has been on a political roller coaster ride in some countries, changing drastically as new regimes come to power. The 1964 constitution of Afghanistan guaranteed women the right to education. However, by 1978, a struggle arose regarding Western influences. Having women receiving an education and moving freely about in public was seen as a slippery slope that would lead the country to certain destruction. Under the Taliban, some girls' schools were closed and converted into Islamic seminaries. With such antagonism toward allowing girls to have a basic education, it is not surprising that, as of April 2000, there was not a single female student in the fourteen facilities of Kabul University.[8]

Here we face a contradiction between the teachings of Muhammed and actual Islamic practice. Muhammed advocated the right of equal education of men and women, going so far as to command that slave girls be educated. Both men and women attended his lectures, including many female scholars.[9]

Some traditionally hard-line countries are trying to make strides in women's rights and education. For instance, the Iranian parliament passed a bill in January 2001 to overturn a 1985 ban on unmarried women receiving state scholarships to study overseas. However, just days later the bill failed to be ratified by the Guardians' Council, a group of conservative clergy and lawyers that makes sure decisions of parliament do not contradict Islamic teaching. Currently, women are not eligible to receive financial aid for foreign study and can only study abroad with the permission of their male guardians.

American Muslim parents are much more apt to educate their daughters, but many still do not like the Western influence that comes in the public school system. The *New York Times* reported that in 1998 at least 200 private Islamic schools were operating in the United States, according to the Council of Islamic Schools in North America. Muslim schools exist for the same reason that Christian schools exist, to integrate academics with religious teaching. Most of the Muslim schools are at capacity and have to turn away almost as many students as they have enrolled. Muslims in America are now estimated to exceed 5 million, with a diverse ethnic makeup of African-Americans, Indians, Pakistanis, Bangladeshis, Arabs, Africans, Iranians, Turks, Southeast Asians, Western European Americans, and Hispanics. In the U.S., Muslims may soon outnumber Jews, making them the second largest religious group.[10] Immigrant families from conservative Muslim countries have created a demand for separate girls' schools because they do not want their daughters to mix with boys, especially at the junior high and high school levels.

Because Muslim schools are an American melting pot for Islamic cultures and traditions, the next generation will probably have a more unified belief system. Each family's cultural background will continue to influence the children in Muslim schools, but an Americanized Islam will emerge. The growth of Islam in the U.S. and Canada suggests that Muslim schools will become more common in urban areas. If we are going to reach Muslims, we must be aware of who is in our neighborhoods and what they believe.

INHERITANCE

Inheritance laws are yet another way to ensure that women remain in their prescribed role. "A male gets one portion equal to twice that of the female" (surah 4:11). A son is given more because he is expected to take care of his female relatives. Islam goes by the rule that "gain is commensurate with liability." Because daughters are not required to provide for and defend others, they do not receive as much inheritance as the male members of the family.

Some countries—including Pakistan, Syria, and Egypt—do not give daughters any share of inheritances. The stricter laws are designed to keep land ownership within a family upon the marriage of the daughter.

FAMILY

Marriage and motherhood are automatic assumptions in the lives of girls from a very early age. A young woman's identity is largely based on her future as a wife and child bearer. As we have already discovered, the birth of sons is paramount in the family. Shaukat Omari, a Pakistani cleric, sums up the purpose of a family: "It is within the family that man, the most noble of all creatures, according to the Islamic concept of life, is brought up."[11] A son gives value and meaning to a woman within her community.

The *ailah*, or extended family, is the hub of Islamic life. The *ailah* usually consists of father, mother, unmarried children, married sons and their wives and children, and unmarried or widowed paternal aunts. Three or four generations may live together under one roof. Some families choose to live in separate homes but in close proximity. Muslims and Christians both believe that the strength of a people comes from the strength of the family. The *Qur'an* discusses the family and the importance of its interdependence in several places (surahs 4:176; 8:41; 16:90; 17:26; 24:22.)

Children reap benefits from living in an extended family. There is no such thing as a single-parent home. If death or divorce has affected a home, plenty of other family members are available to fill the shoes of the absent parent. Discipline is not as big an issue as in other cultures, because there are numerous adults in the home to reinforce the rules and boundaries.

Women are the foundation of the home and its operation. Older women in the home model the role that girls are to emulate later in life. Young girls are often found in the kitchen with the women of the family, learning the basics of meal preparation. By age seven, girls are encouraged to join the women in *salaat* (daily prayers). *Salaat* becomes mandatory upon reaching adulthood, which starts for girls with the onset of their menstrual cycle and for boys by the beginning of puberty.

A daughter learns to give deference to all male members of her household. She is expected to give total obedience without the least protest and to be led wherever her father and brothers wish.[12] The men in her extended family are the only male members of society that a girl is exposed to from puberty onward, or maybe earlier, depending on her country of birth and the sect of Islam her family practices. This separation is designed to protect young people from sexual temptations and immoral activity, as well as to maintain the mystery of the opposite sex until after marriage.

Is a girl's worth diminished if she chooses a life that does not include motherhood? What can we as Christians offer a young woman who does not desire to fulfill her prescribed role in Islamic society? First Corinthians 7:34–35 describes the role of a single Christian woman: "There is a difference between a wife and a virgin. The unmarried woman cares about the things of the Lord, that she may be holy both in body and in spirit. But she who is married cares about the things of the world—how she may please her husband. And this I say for your own profit, not that I may put a leash on you, but for what is proper, and that you may serve the Lord without distraction" (NKJV).

Women with the gift of singleness play a unique role in Christendom. Many godly single women have spent a lifetime faithfully serving the Lord and have often challenged me to a closer walk with Jesus Christ. As Christian women, our fulfillment comes from God alone. The realization that no other relationship or position can fill the void that is made for God leads us to contentment in whatever path God chooses for our lives, including the call to singleness.

MARRIAGE

From the protected and secluded environment of the extended family, Muslim daughters are sent into marriage. In many cases, the bride and groom do not meet until the day the wedding contract is signed. In Islam, marriage is as much a joining of two families as it is a joining of two individuals. For this reason, the family has a large amount of participation in the choice of marriage partners.[13]

CONSENT

The issue of a woman's consent *(ijab)* varies among Muslim cultures. It is generally believed that a father has the right to marry his daughter to anyone he wishes, without her consent. The only stipulation on the father is that the proposed groom be suitable. To be regarded as unsuitable, a prospective husband might be from the wrong social status or religious sect, or the age difference might be regarded as too great.[14] If the woman feels that a husband is unsuitable on some grounds, she can apply for nullification. Otherwise, the marriage stands.

In contrast, parents have little or no say about a son's choice of spouse. Men may seek a wife that pleases them and with whom they desire to live and have a family, so long as the girl's parents do not object. The same degree of personal happiness is not afforded to daughters. The reasoning behind arranged marriages of daughters is that they need help to marry wisely so that they will be cared for, as the role of wife and mother typically does not include an income.

Christian parents share the concern that their children marry wisely. During the typical dating years, parents guide their daughters to discern the type of temperament and personality that would best suit them in a spouse. A Christian girl should learn to ask questions that reveal the depth of spirituality of those she dates. A girl who has dedicated her life to pleasing the Lord Jesus commits to dating only Christian young men who have at least the same level of commitment that she has. When a dating relationship has this kind of foundation, security and personal happiness are by-products for husbands and wives.

Not all Muslims accept the conclusion that a father or guardian has sole authority in arranging marriage for his daughters. Some think the daughter's consent to the proposed spouse is necessary. Conservative Muslims say it is admirable for a father to consult his daughter, but it is not required. A woman's right to choose or reject a potential spouse is largely nullified by the fact that a male relative (usually the father) must arrange the marriage contract.

This presents another interesting dichotomy in Islam. The overwhelming evidence from Islamic texts supports the right of young women to choose or approve of their spouses. The *Qur'an* does not deal with the issue of consent, but it is mentioned more than once in the Hadithic literature. Abu Huraira reports that Muhammed said, "A matron should not be given in marriage except after consulting her; and a virgin should not be given in marriage except after her permission." When asked how a woman's permission would be known, Muhammed answered, "Her silence [indicates her permission]."

Imam Ahmad reported that Aishah said that a woman went to Muhammed after her father had offered her to his nephew in marriage. The woman's objection to the marriage was not based on the man's character or his social standing. Muhammed let the woman decide by saying, "If you do not, no one has the right to force you to accept it."

The Ayatollah Ruholla Mussaui Khomeini (1900–1989) consulted his daughter, Zahra, when he began to look for a husband for her. She was an educated young woman, although not in Iran's state-run school system. Khomeini chose religious men to educate Zahra at home. When her studies were completed, he approached her with names of possible husbands. She turned down the first three he suggested and finally agreed to the fourth. After each suggestion he would say, "It's up to you."

MARRIAGE OF MINORS

Although some Muslim women are granted the right to give consent to marriage, others are not. Unfortunately, many of the latter are children.

Prior to Ayatollah Khomeini's return to Iran in 1975, child brides were illegal under the shah's Family Protection Law. When the Islamic Republic came to power in 1979, its resurgence of Islamic fundamentalism nullified the Family Protection Law, and nine-year-old girls were legally eligible for marriage.

Why so young a minimum age? The answer is that Muhammed himself took Aishah, the six-year-old daughter of his closest advisor, Abu Bakr, as his third wife. He cohabited with her from the time she was nine. In defense of Muhammed, some Muslims argue that if a girl was promised in marriage at a young age, the marriage might not be consummated until she was older. It is not at all unusual for the marriage contract (aqd nikah) to be signed for some time before the wedding party and consummation of the marriage. After the urs (wedding), the bride moves to the home of her new husband. In the case of Aishah, the Hadith of Sahih al-Bukhari, the collection of ahadith most widely accepted by Islamic scholars, says that Muhammed was in his fifties when he consummated the marriage with his nine-year-old bride: "Narrated A'isha that the Prophet wrote the marriage contract with her when she was six years old and he consummated his marriage when she was nine years old. Hisham said: 'I have been informed that A'isha remained with the Prophet for nine years [i.e. till his death]'" (hadith 7.65).

> Narrated A'isha: The prophet engaged me when I was a girl of six [years]. We went to Medina and stayed at the home of Bani-al-Harith bin Kharzraj. Then I got ill and my hair fell down. Later on my hair grew [again] and my mother, Um Ruman, came to me while I was playing in a swing with some of my girl friends. She called me, and I went to her, not knowing what she wanted to do to me. She caught me by the hand

and made me stand at the door of the house. I was breathless then, and when my breathing became all right, she took some water and rubbed my face and head with it. Then she took me into the house. There in the house I saw some Ansari women who said, "Best wishes and Allah's blessing and a good luck." Then she entrusted me to them and they prepared me [for the marriage]. Unexpectedly, Allah's messenger came to me in the forenoon and my mother handed me over to him, and at that time I was a girl of nine years of age. (hadith 5:234)

Arab custom held that a girl who had her first menstrual cycle was considered an adult. Aishah reportedly came of age at age nine, which made her able to consummate her arranged marriage with Muhammed and move to his home. Because Muhammed's life is to be emulated, faithful Muslims in Iran and numerous other countries have followed the precedent of Muhammed's marriage to Aishah.

The onset of puberty as a signal to a girl's readiness to marry is questionable, at best. Menstruation is merely the physical sign that a female body is capable of reproduction. Emotional maturity takes a great deal longer to develop. Although some girls begin menstruating as young as age nine, most are between eleven and twelve years old. Their bodies are beginning to shows signs of womanhood, but they are not physically developed enough at that point to adequately handle intercourse or pregnancy. Girls younger than fifteen years old have more spontaneous abortions and stillbirths and are four times as likely to die from pregnancy-related causes than is a woman over twenty years of age.[15]

In twenty-first-century Iran, it is still legal for a nine-year-old girl to marry, although a law passed in June 2002 now stipulates that she cannot marry without her parents' permission. For that privilege she must wait until the age of thirteen. This law only affects girls who wish to marry without the consent of their parents. It in no way offers protection from an arranged marriage of a child to an adult male.

In many parts of the Muslim world, the marriage of child brides is supported. In Nepal, 40 percent of all marriages are consummated when the bride is younger than fourteen years old. A survey in Calcutta found women who had married between the ages of seven and fifteen. Half of those women spoke of forced sexual intercourse.[16] A 1993 UNICEF survey of five thousand women in Rajasthen (India) recorded that 56 percent of the women were married before the age of fifteen and 17 percent were younger than ten years old.[17] The notion that marrying daughters off as child brides was only a seventh-century practice is clearly mistaken. The marriage of child brides is alive and well in the twenty-first century.

The issue of arranged marriages for young girls has set off a battle between clerics, who see the practice as a means of warding off promiscuity, and reformists, who are fighting for women's rights. The reformists within Islam have much to be concerned about when it comes to the well-being of child brides. One writer relates the story of a friend's thirteen-year-old sister, who lived under a strict Islamic code in their homeland. When the girl's breasts began to develop, her parents decided to stop her schooling and marry her off. The intended spouse was a forty-five-year-old grandfather of seven, the husband of two women. On the wedding night, the young girl was confused and appalled by her husband's sexual advances. When she resisted, she was raped and died on her wedding night.[18]

Some fathers try to impose outward sanctions on their daughters to secure their chastity and preserve the family's honor and the respect of their community. This can be seen in the efforts made by one Ivory Coast Muslim father. Twelve-year-old Azara would often leave the house and return hours later without offering any information on her whereabouts. Once her father tied her up, burned her back with a piece of iron, then locked her in a room for three days without food. He never sent Azara to school, because if girls went to a "modern" school, they might meet people who would drive them from their traditions. Educated girls "argue with their parents. They start asking questions and do not want to marry until they are nineteen or twenty." As soon as he married Azara off to a forty-year-old man, "I got peace of mind. She was no longer my problem," said the father.[19]

Groups such as the Forum on the Rights of Women and Girls in

Marriage are seeking to stamp out the practice of child marriages. Countries that allow the marriage of little girls in order to protect their chastity are stealing their childhood. Girls will not be adequately protected until hearts change within the culture.

The Bible speaks of the nature of the human heart. "For out of the heart come evil thoughts, murder, adultery, sexual immorality, theft, false testimony, slander" (Matthew 15:19 NIV). The heart shows the true inner person. "As water reflects a face, so a man's heart reflects the man" (Proverbs 27:19 NIV). How then does a heart change? "Therefore, if anyone is in Christ, he is a new creation; the old has gone, the new has come!" (2 Corinthians 5:17 NIV). Having a personal relationship with the living Lord Jesus and seeking to please him with every action is the only way to live a truly moral life.

HONOR

In Islamic societies, the honor of a daughter, as well as that of her father and her brothers, depends on her chastity. As we have already discussed, that honor is sometimes "upheld" by marrying the daughter off before she can dishonor the male members of her family. Others choose to safeguard their daughters' morality by attempting to lessen her sexual pleasure through genital mutilation.

Clitoridectomy is a form of genital mutilation that involves removing all or part or the clitoris. Infibulation, or pharaonic circumcision, is a more extreme procedure. It includes clitoridectomy and adds the cutting away of the labia and the sealing of the wound to cover the vagina, leaving only a small opening for urination and menstruation.

In Eritrea, on the coast of Ethiopia, an eight-year-old girl was held down while her clitoris was scraped away with an unclean knife and then sealed with acacia thorns. Some time later, on her wedding night, her husband used a dagger to cut his way into what was left of her genitals.[20]

An estimated 135 million girls and women have undergone genital mutilation.[21] It is a common practice in Africa and in the Middle East, and is practiced by Muslims in Indonesia, Sri Lanka, Malaysia, India,

Egypt, Oman, Yemen, and the United Arab Emirates. Today, one in five Muslim girls lives in a community that sanctions some type of interference with her genitals. Until a few years ago, it was traditional in the Buraimi Oasis region of the United Arab Emirates to remove about one-eighth of an inch from the clitoris of all six-year-old girls.[22]

In the Muslim area of Eritrea, women were told that such practices were written in the Qur'an. "My mother, my grandmother and my great grandmother all told me it was right, that without it a woman wouldn't be able to control herself, that she would end up a prostitute," said one victim.[23] Because the women were not educated, they could not read the Qur'an for themselves to discover that genital mutilation is never condoned.

The physical results of infibulation are long-term and serious. They can include chronic urinary tract infections, stones in the bladder and urethra, kidney damage, reproductive tract infections resulting from obstructed menstrual flow, pelvic infections, infertility, excessive scar tissue, keloids (raised, irregularly shaped, progressively enlarging scars) and dermoid cysts.

The psychological effects are more difficult to categorize than the physical. Imagine being brought up in a society that assumes you are completely incapable of restraining yourself sexually. We see here a contradiction in Islam. In some respects, women are to be honored above all, yet they are trusted so little that they must be surgically altered and kept in isolation in order to be controlled.

Sexual temptation has existed since the origin of sin. However, women (and men) need not be slaves to their physical urges. It is an act of the will to dismiss thoughts that would lead to immoral behavior and to replace them with God-honoring thoughts. When Christian women choose to participate in conduct that is not in keeping with Scripture, the honor of our heavenly Father is at stake. God has given us all that is necessary to be positive witnesses to His power rather than a smear on His holy name.

"And I will pray the Father, and He will give you another Helper, that He may abide with you forever—the Spirit of truth, whom the world cannot receive, because it neither sees Him nor knows Him;

but you know Him, for He dwells with you and will be in you" (John 14:16–17 NKJV).

As Christians, we believe we have the choice to submit to the Holy Spirit within us or to let the flesh control our actions. Women who are subjected to genital mutilation are not given the opportunity to simply preserve their chastity, because they are not given the opportunity to fail. Instead, the assumption is that moral failure is almost assured unless steps are taken to prevent it.

If such extreme measures are taken to protect family honor, what happens when that honor is violated? Although Islamic belief holds the role of females in highest regard, many Islamic societies turn a violent hand toward young women when family honor is at stake. An extreme example of this violence occurred in June 2002 in Meerwala, Pakistan. The incident began when an eleven-year-old boy walked with a girl from a different tribe without a chaperone. In Pakistan, crimes to dignity are not handled by Pakistani law but rather by tribal council. The council ruled that the girl in question had been dishonored and ordered as punishment the rape of the boy's eighteen-year-old sister, in order to shame the family. Four members of the council took turns raping the young woman while hundreds of people stood outside the hut cheering.

"I wept. I cried. I said I taught the holy *Qur'an* to children in the village, therefore don't punish me for a crime which was not committed by me. But they tore my clothes and raped me one by one," she said.[24]

Where is the honor in such an action? Dishonoring the older girl did not restore the honor of the younger girl.

Girls living under a strict Islamic code have much to fear regarding their physical well-being. Every year, about forty Palestinian women die at the hands of their fathers and brothers in so-called "honor killings" that are intended to wipe away the shame of a female relative's premarital or extramarital sexual relationships.[25]

Honor killings are not found in the *Qur'an* or in the Hadithic literature, but they have become a silent custom in poorer Muslim villages, although many deny that they occur. Is it mere coincidence that girls who are caught in wrong or questionable behavior suddenly disappear or their bodies are found in burned-out cars?

A British photographer captured on film one such execution in July 1977. Saudi princess Misha bint Fahd bin Mohamed was shot in the head six times in a Jeddah parking lot and her male companion beheaded. At the time of the execution, the princess was separated from her husband. The 1980 documentary *Death of a Princess* recounts Misha's story, including the photographs of her murder. Under *sharia* law, a confession by the accused or the testimony of four eyewitnesses is required in order for someone to be convicted of adultery.

The *Qur'an* states, "If any of your women are guilty of lewdness, take the evidence of four [reliable] witnesses from amongst you against them; and if they testify, confine them to houses until death do claim them, or Allah ordain for them some [other] way" (surah 4:15). Neither the princess nor her boyfriend would have been convicted under *sharia* law.

Victoria's story has a much different outcome. She is a wife and mother of two beautiful children in the United States. Every Sunday she and her family attend worship services at the church where she was brought up. Although Victoria had accepted Christ as her Savior when she was seven years old, as a young adult she made immoral choices. At the age of twenty-four, Victoria discovered that she would soon be a single mother. The thought of telling her parents panicked her, not because they would be angry, but because she was ashamed to hurt and disappoint them. Victoria recalls her father's response to the news. "He was stunned," she said. "Then he hugged me and told me he loved me."

Her parents gave her the support she so desperately needed during the pregnancy. They pointed her to God's love and care for her, and encouraged her to return to church and commit to living a life that pleased the Lord Jesus. "Their main concern was that I raise this child around the things of the Lord," she said.

"He never told me he was disappointed," Victoria said of her father. "He only showed love for me and for a baby that came out of order." Victoria had been taught that sexual intercourse is a gift from God to be enjoyed after marriage. She knew that becoming pregnant before marriage was not the order of events that God intended. Victoria's father responded to her with the same patience and mercy he had experienced through the forgiveness of Christ. The unconditional love of her earthly father resulted in spiritual restoration to her heavenly Father.

The God of the Bible is not the author of fear. Can you imagine the response of a young Muslim woman who is told of the forgiveness of Christ and of the freedom He brings to everyday living? Who will tell them that we are each responsible for our actions before the Lord? Who will tell them that only Jesus can pay the penalty for our sinful behavior and that we are not held accountable for the actions of another?

CONCLUSION

As I have researched and written these pages, my thoughts could not help but turn to my own daughter. As a mother, I cannot conceive of her living under the constraints of a Muslim society. Most of these girls have never heard that Jesus loves them and that He died for their sin and rose from the dead to provide an abundant life. While they wait for someone to tell them of Jesus, many are brutalized physically, married off young, and left to live in ignorance.

What opportunity has God placed in front of you? Do you have a Muslim neighbor with whom you can begin to build a relationship and model the freedom found in Christ Jesus? Do you know of a short-term mission trip to Muslim refugees? We as Christians cannot sit back and let feminist groups and secular child advocates fight alone for the plight of millions of girls behind the veil of Islam.

NOTES

1. Nicole Gaouette, "Voices from behind the veil," http://www.csmonitor.com/2001/1219/pls3-wogi.html (20 August 2002).

2. W. Robertson Smith, *Kinship & Marriage in Early Arabia* (London: Adam and Charles Black, 1903), 292.

3. "Answering Islam: A Christian-Muslim Dialog," http://www.answering-islam.org/ (17 August 2002).

4. Shaukat Omari, *Islam: In the Light of the Final Testament* (Karachi, Pakistan: Taurus, 1992), 268.

5. Geraldine Brooks, *Nine Parts of Desire* (New York: Anchor, 1995), 149.

6. "Country by Country Statistics of Muslim Populations," http://www.adherents.com/Na_321.html#2058 (6 October 2002).

7. Brooks, *Nine Parts of Desire*, 148–50.

8. Reported by the Revolutionary Association of the Women of Afghanistan, http://rawa.fancymarketing.net/uni.htm (9 October 2002).

9. Lois Lamya'al Faruqi, *Women, Muslim Society and Islam* (Plainfield, Ind.: American Trust Publications, 1988), 37.

10. Elizabeth J. Plantz "Bridging the Gap: Islam in America," http://www.islamfortoday.com/library.htm (12 October 2002).

11. Omari, *Islam: In the Light of the Final Testament*, 267.

12. "Answering Islam: A Christian-Muslim Dialog," http://www.answering-islam.org/ (17 August 2002).

13. Faruqi, *Women, Muslim Society and Islam*, 64.

14. Omari, *Islam: In the Light of the Final Testament*, 123.

15. http://www.vso.org.uk/publications/orbit/72/fears.htm, p. 7 (17 October 2002).

16. Ibid.

17. Varsha Bhosle, "Paedophilia and the Muslim Board," http://www.rediff.com/news/2002/jul/01varsha.htm (17 October 2002).

18. "Answering Islam: A Christian-Muslim Dialog," http://www.answering-islam.org/ (17 August 2002).

19. Stephen Buckley, "Wedded to Tradition: Marriage at Puberty," Washington Post Foreign News Service, http://www.washingtonpost.com/wp-srv/inatl/longterm/africanlives/ivory/ivory.htm (17 October 2002).

20. Brooks, *Nine Parts of Desire*, 33–34.

21. http://www.amnesty.org/ailib/intcam/femgen/fgm1.htm#a1 (3 October 2002).

22. Brooks, *Nine Parts of Desire*, 36.

23. Ibid., 34.

24. Khalid Tanveer, "Tribal rape sparks outrage, probe," The Associated Press, *Palm Beach Post*, 4 July 2002, 21A.

25. Brooks, *Nine Parts of Desire*, 49–50.

8

PROTECTED PROPERTY

Wives in Islam

Kathy L. Sibley

As a former Middle East missionary, Kathy L. Sibley brings
a world of experience and prudence to an often-volatile subject. Rather than engage in combative argument, Sibley offers a sympathetic view into the world of Muslim wives and
their deepest needs. Her heart for women is evident in this
often-moving and poignant chapter. By her own admission,
Sibley's greatest joy in the ministry has been that of a pastor's
wife and counselor to women.

Before the dissolution of the Soviet Union in the early 1990s, Nurjan
earnestly started to seek an experience with God. In those days, the only
religious people she knew were the *tauips* (mystics) and the Islamic leaders. After observing their hypocritical lifestyles, she became cynical about
the teachings handed down from her elders. In desperation, she sincerely prayed, asking the true God to reveal Himself to her. She continued to pray for more than two years, asking God to show her the truth.
The day she and I met, hope leaped in her heart that perhaps God had
sent me in answer to her prayer. The Holy Spirit had specifically prepared her heart to lower her prejudices against "white" people. In several of her dreams she saw white, Russian-looking people speaking Kazak,
preparing Kazak tea, and identifying with Kazak culture. She felt these
persons could be trusted to help her find the way of life.

The story astounded me. Living among a people cut off from the gospel, missionaries, Scripture, and from everything Christian, this young woman had cried out to know the one, true God—and He had heard her. A shocking truth dawned on me that night. The members of God's church may not be the only ones praying that God would send workers into the harvest. Those praying the most fervently may be the very same ones who themselves are the harvest.[1]

God is working in the hearts of Muslim women, and He has called His children to join Him in His work. As we consider the circumstances of Muslim women in general, and wives in particular, the point should not be missed that, in their hearts, *all* women yearn to know "the way and the truth and the life" (John 14:6). *All* women yearn to make a difference in the world. *All* women yearn to be loved and to love. And there are "voices behind the veil" calling for help.

How do we tune our ears to hear those heart cries? Certainly, part of the answer lies in seeking to understand the societal pressures and cultural expectations of those for whom we are concerned. Thus, we turn our attention to Islam and to the plight of women who are entrenched in that world.

Identifying a prototypical Muslim woman is more elusive than the quest for the Holy Grail. Not only is it dangerous to generalize—it is also impossible to come up with more than a caricature of what she might look like, what she experiences, or what freedoms she does or does not enjoy. According to C. M. Amal,

> The majority of Muslim women live in developing countries, areas of conflict, war zones, or countries prone to catastrophic natural disasters. The overwhelming masses of Muslims live in abject poverty, which is aggravated by high birth rates. Muslim women live in a kaleidoscope of political systems, from brutal dictatorships to constitutional monarchies. But the *umma* [essence] of Islam is spiritual, and this allegiance transcends national boundaries.[2]

Precisely because the essence of Islam is spiritual, the most helpful perspective may be derived from statements made in the *Qurʾan* and

Hadith and by authoritative commentators. Certainly the interpretation of selected passages might be debated, but these passages speak fairly clearly about the issues encountered by Muslim women. For our discussion, four of those issues demand special attention: genetic inferiority, polygamy, marital punishment, and divorce.

GENETIC INFERIORITY

Islam teaches that wives are possessions and women are inherently inferior to men. Surah 3:14 states: "Fair in the eyes of men is the love of things they covet: women and sons; heaped-up hoards of gold and silver." The status of wives is further illuminated by surah 2:223: "Your wives are as a tilth [field to be plowed] unto you, so approach your tilth when and how ye will." Again, *Kanz-el-ʾUmmal Hadith* 22.858 says: "Wives are playthings, so take your pick." It is clear that wives are viewed as sex objects—toys for personal gratification. How contrary is the picture of marriage in 1 Peter 3:7: "Husbands, in the same way be considerate as you live with your wives, and treat them with respect as the weaker partner and as heirs with you of the gracious gift of life, so that nothing will hinder your prayers" (NIV).

Husbands are urged to dwell with their wives in an understanding way, to dote on them, and to devote their lives to them. Only in this context can sexual expression become a reflection of the spiritual oneness and dynamism between two people who respect and sacrificially love one another.

Islam teaches that women are inherently inferior to men. In the *Qurʾan*, surah 2:228 states that "women shall have rights similar to the rights against them, according to what is equitable; but men have a degree [of advantage] over them."

In surah 4:34, the roles of men and women are outlined: "Men are the protectors and maintainers of women, because Allah has given the one more [strength] than the other, and because they support them from their means. Therefore the righteous women are devoutly obedient, and guard in [the husband's] absence what Allah would have them guard."

Muhammed clarified the position further when he stated that women are genetically and legally inferior. "The Prophet said, 'Isn't the witness of a woman equal to half of that of a man?' The women said, 'Yes.' He said, 'This is because of the deficiency of the woman's mind'" (hadith 3.48.826). Not only is a man's wife considered inferior, but she is also considered detrimental to her husband. "Allah's apostle said, 'If at all there is bad omen, it is in the horse, the woman, and the house . . . after me I have not left any affliction more harmful to men than women'" (hadith 7.62.32–33).

Has this position gone unchallenged? Is it so pervasive in society that no one ever dares speak against such denigration? Nawal El Sadawi, a female Muslim writer, states that in Islam

> The institution of marriage remained very different for men to what it was for women, and the rights accorded to husbands were distinct from those accorded to wives. In fact it is probably not accurate to use the term "rights of the woman" since a woman under the Islamic system of marriage has no human rights unless we consider that a slave has rights under a slave system. Marriage, in so far as women are concerned, is just like slavery to the slave, or the chains of serfdom to the serf.[3]

In stark contrast, Jesus, whose cultural setting bore similarity to the Middle East of the twenty-first century, elevated women in a revolutionary way. Jesus treated women as equally created in the image of God and, as such, equal recipients of God's grace and forgiveness. Consequently, the roles of husbands and wives in marriage, though differentiated, are nonetheless roles in which both partners share a basic equality of value and corresponding rights and responsibilities.

POLYGAMY

In approaching a discussion of polygamy, the inevitable question emerges, Is polygamy a "divine right" or an exception to the rule? Without question, the *Qur'an* permits a man to marry up to four wives.

Surah 4:3 enjoins: "If ye fear that ye shall not be able to deal justly with the orphans, marry women of your choice, two, or three, or four; but if ye fear that ye shall not be able to deal justly [with them], then only one, or [a captive] that your right hands possess. That will be more suitable, to prevent you from doing injustice." One commentator suggests that the form of the text is stylistically ambiguous. The writer departed from a whole number to approximate numbers in Arabic, thus giving wiggle room to those so inclined to take more wives. The suggestion may be viable, since at the time the verse was penned, Muhammed, himself, was legally married to nine wives.[4]

What is the "injustice" to which the *Qur'an* refers? The *Qur'an* admonishes the man with two or more wives to be scrupulously fair among them. Surah 4:129 says: "Ye are never able to be fair and just as between women, even if it is your ardent desire: But turn not away [from a woman] altogether, so as to leave her [as it were] hanging [in the air]. If ye come to a friendly understanding, and practice self-restraint, Allah is Oft-forgiving, Most Merciful." Citing Tuffaha, an Islamic commentator, Rafiqul-Haqq and P. Newton conclude: "The majority of the commentators agreed that 'the equality in Q. 4:3 is concerned with apportioning time and money, while the equality mentioned in Q. 3:129 is concerned with the affection and love of the man towards his wives.'"[5] They further argue that Muhammed was not impartial in his affections toward his wives, for he loved Aishah more than any of the rest.

In addition to the permission for polygamy given by Muhammed, some leading Muslim scholars have also endorsed the practice. One such justification is offered by Ghazali: "Some men have such a compelling sexual desire that one woman is not sufficient to protect them [from adultery]. Such men therefore preferably marry more than one woman and may have up to four wives."[6] In addition to four wives, a man is also permitted to take concubines and slaves, according to what their right hand possesses.

Debbie Bartlotti, who lived and worked for thirteen years among women on the border between Pakistan and Afghanistan, adds the following observation:

> Two wizened old women dressed in black are the matriarchs.
> . . . These women and a third woman now dead shared one
> husband. . . . They were shaking their heads in disbelief after
> hearing that in the West men would be put in jail for having
> more than one wife. They looked wide-eyed at one another
> and at me and spoke with sincere logic: "What if the husband
> is unhappy with his wife?" "What if she can have no children?"
> Then in a gasping finale, "What if she can have no sons?"[7]

Though these matriarchs apparently survived the conflict of earlier years, jealousy, envy, quarrels and conflict all too often exist among
multiple wives. Even accounts of polygamy in the Bible record such
strife, as between Sarah and Hagar (Genesis 16; 21:8–14). It should be
noted that God's blueprint for the institution of marriage is one man
and one woman for life. Deviations from this blueprint were never
sanctioned by God and were always accompanied by harmful consequences. The Holy One of Israel never tolerates sin, nor is His design
ever compromised. In 1 Corinthians 7:2–3, we read: "Let each man
have his own wife, and let each woman have her own husband. Let the
husband render to his wife the affection due her, and likewise also the
wife to her husband" (NKJV).

Islam is extremely inventive for men who believe they cannot be impartial, giving the option known as "temporary marriage" or mut'a (see
pp. 77–78 and 114–15). Temporary marriages are personal contracts between a man and a woman, who may be an acquaintance or even a stranger.
In it the man offers the woman a sum of money in exchange for a designated period of marriage. The man provides her with housing and all
other necessities. In exchange, she commits to satisfy his sexual demands
whenever he wants, without hindrance. She is exclusively his for the du-
ration of the contract. When the contract expires, the man can either pay
her and release her or renew the contract for another term. Temporary
marriages were historically practiced when men went off to war, leaving
their wives behind. As they relocated, they would meet women with whom
they would contract for sexual gratification. The practice was also common among men of business and commerce.

The custom of *mut'a* is complex and has wide variations in the different sects of Islam. As every Muslim knows, the *Shi'a* sect practices this contractual marriage, but Sunni Muslims do not, in spite of its admissibility in the *Qur'an*. The *Qur'an* definitely sanctions it, and Muhammed not only agreed to it but also practiced this type of liaison.

By contrast, we read in 1 Thessalonians 4:3–6: "For this is the will of God, your sanctification; that is, that you abstain from sexual immorality; that each of you know how to possess his own vessel in sanctification and honor, not in lustful passion . . . and that no man transgress and defraud his brother in the matter because the Lord is the avenger in all these things" (NASB). In Christ, we find a higher law, a deeper purity, and a richer passion.

MARITAL PUNISHMENT

Once Muhammed was asked: "What rights does the woman have with the man?" He replied, "He should feed her if he eats, clothe her when he dresses, avoid disfiguring her or beating her excessively or abandoning her except at home." From the prophet's own lips, then, the standard of Islam is revealed.

Beyond the question of rights, though, is an issue of far greater concern. Within the *Qur'an* is a jarring admonition concerning marital punishment. The *Qur'an* plainly commands men to beat their wives as soon as they show any sign of disobedience to male authority. Surah 4:34 says: "As to those women on whose part you fear disloyalty and ill-conduct, admonish them [first], [next], refuse to share their beds, [and last] beat them [lightly]."

The occasion in which surah 4:34 was revealed sheds light on the meaning of that verse, which "was revealed in connection with a woman who complained to Muhammed that her husband slapped her on the face (which was still marked by the slap). At first the Prophet said to her: 'Get even with him,' but then added: 'Wait until I think about it.' Later on, the above verse was revealed, after which the Prophet said: 'We wanted one thing but Allah wanted another, and what Allah wanted is best.'"[8]

The translator of Mishkat Al-Masabih noted that beating the wife mildly is "allowed in four cases: (1) When she does not wear fineries though wanted by the husband, (2) When she is called for sexual intercourse and she refuses without any lawful excuse, (3) When she is ordered to take a bath [to clean herself] from impurities for prayer and she refuses, and (4) When she goes abroad without permission of her husband."[9]

The man who fears rebelliousness in his wife must admonish her first. If that remedy is not effective, the husband has the right to desert her sexually. If that effort is ineffective, he has the right to beat her, providing he does not break her bones or shed blood.

A man's right to beat his wife is not relegated to the distant past. According to a report in the *Guardian Weekly:* "In 1987 an Egyptian court, following an interpretation of the *Qur'an* proposed by the Syndicate of Arab Lawyers, ruled that a husband had the duty to educate his wife and therefore the right to punish her as he wished."[10] The woman, however, cannot resort to such measures, if she fears rebelliousness in her husband. The wife is expected to satisfy the desires of her husband at all costs, and is to regard his wishes as sacrosanct. In fact, the obedience of the wife to her husband is a critical prerequisite that shows her piety and guarantees her eternal destiny. Her response to him approaches worship. Muhammed said: "Had I ordered anybody to prostrate before anyone, I would have ordered women to prostrate before their husbands on account of men's rights over the women ordained by Allah."

Debbie Bartlotti, a nurse clinician and midwife working for an Afghan clinic and hospital, has seen gross examples of physical abuse and neglect firsthand: "A large nomad woman dressed in a colorful velvet dress flowing down to the floor came for an antenatal exam. As I listened to her chest, I noticed huge black and blue marks all over her back and buttocks. Through the small braids ringing her face, I heard a quiet voice utter one word, the Pashto word for *brick.*"[11]

Such incidents cause one's mind and emotions to reel. Muslim wives have few defenders and little or no access to a protective legal system. What hope can be offered? Without question, some are working clandestinely to bring healing and hope to the victims of such beatings, but there is one ultimate answer—the power of the gospel of Jesus Christ. Only by that power can such cruelty and inhumanity be overcome.

The admonition to husbands and wives in Ephesians 5 is in stark contrast to the aforementioned brutality. The behavior of husbands and wives is to be governed by a desire to honor, serve, and submit to one another. Submission to authority is a cardinal principle of authentic Christian faith. In the Ephesians passage, it is worth noting that the Greek verb form that is translated in English by the word *submit* means "to submit oneself *voluntarily* to another." Herein lies what may be the greatest difference between the life of a Muslim wife who is *subjected by* her husband, and a Christian wife who, under the authority of the Lord Jesus, *voluntarily submits* to her husband's loving leadership. The marriage relationship is to be characterized by mutual respect and sacrificial, redemptive love, rather than by ruthless power, domination, and control. Husbands are to model selfless love—a love that seeks the best for another. Likewise, submission is a gift that wives give in return.

DIVORCE

It is common knowledge among all sects of Islam that a man can divorce his wife for any reason. According to Islamic law, a man may divorce his wife by saying: "You are divorced . . . you are divorced . . . you are divorced," or "You are divorced by three" in a moment of anger. But suppose after the man cools off, or after a sumptuous meal, he regrets his hasty action and relents. Is it simply a matter of "forgive and forget"? No, for according to surah 2:230, "If a husband divorces his wife [irrevocably], he cannot, after that, remarry her until after she has married another husband and he has divorced her. In that case there is no blame on either of them if they reunite, provided they feel that they can keep the limits ordained by Allah. Such are the limits ordained by Allah, which He makes plain to those who understand."

There are a number of classifications. For example, a man can divorce his wife twice without her knowledge and take her back. However, if he divorces her the first time and leaves her, he can return to her without consulting her. This is known as "minor separation." If he divorces her the second time, both husband and wife must remain separate for a specified period. If, during the separation, there is not a change of heart, the wife is required to observe a probationary period of three months in the event that she is pregnant. This is known as a "major separation." If the wife is pregnant, the husband must assume the expenses if he insists on leaving her. Only after the birth will they divorce. If she then returns to her husband (which is likely for economic reasons) and he divorces her again, she is no longer legally his wife. If the parties insist on returning to one another, the woman is first required to consummate a marriage with another man before she can remarry her first husband.

Contrast these regulations with the clear teaching of Scripture regarding divorce in Deuteronomy 24:1–4. Specifically, verse 4 mandates that "her former husband who sent her away is not allowed to take her again to be his wife, since she has been defiled; for that is an *abomination* before the LORD, and you shall not bring sin on the land which the LORD your God gives you as an inheritance" (NASB).

Although a Muslim woman cannot pronounce divorce like a man, she can obtain one through an arbitrator. This process is called *khul,* and the woman asks for divorce in lieu of returning her bridal money or any other gift to the husband.[12] Of this practice, Bartlotti gives insight into the role of women in Islamic society:

> A Muslim woman's essential identity is determined by her relationships with men—her father, her husband, and her family. She is not defined autonomously, but in relationship to males, for whom she functions as a symbol of both honor and of Islam. Just as a Muslim man relates to Almighty God and his decrees—with submission, meekness and obedience, his life directed toward a Divine center and revolving around Allah—so a woman is to relate to a man: with submission, obedience and meekness, her life circling his. In this sense,

Muslim women symbolize the essence of Islam—and in this we find the roots of their social vulnerability.[13]

The revolutionary truth is that while no woman's "essential identity" should be determined by her relationships with men, it *should* be determined by her relationship with the God-Man, Jesus the Messiah. Only as she relates to Him in saving faith can she truly experience the freedom for which she longs. Only as she experiences intimacy with Him, can she truly know the liberating joy of serving others for His sake.

CONCLUSION

One of the most perplexing and hotly debated topics is the role of wives in Islamic society. Opinions are strong and varied. Commentaries are conflicting and diverse. There are no simple analyses. There are no simple solutions. In spite of the wide divergence of cultural expression, socioeconomic status, and adherence to tradition within the global community of Muslim women, there is a unifying framework that is provided by the *Qur'an* as the source and language of the faith. Regardless of the latitude that might be given, the shadow of the *Qur'an* falls on them all.

And herein lies our greatest challenge as witnesses for the truth: We must effectively communicate the message of the Cross, the message that the eternal, transcendent, omnipotent, Creator God became flesh so that He could come into our world and experience what we experience—our alienation and separation—and do what only He could do to redeem and love that world back to Himself. Not only must we effectively communicate that message with our mouths, but we should also incarnate that message in our lives. Only the love of the Lord Jesus Christ could constrain us to do what we are helpless to do otherwise.

As we seek to tune our ears to the "voices behind the veil," may the love we have for the Lord make us dependable in sharing our faith with women who are prisoners—not of an oppressive society, nor of a dictatorial government, but of sin.

We hold the key.

"The Spirit of the Sovereign LORD is on me, because the LORD has anointed me to preach good news to the poor. He has sent me to bind up the brokenhearted, to proclaim freedom for the captives and release from darkness for the prisoners" (Isaiah 61:1 NIV).

Thus was the mission of Jesus, the one who said, "As the Father has sent Me, I also send you" (John 20:21 NKJV).

NOTES

1. Ron Coody, *Fields of Gold: Planting a Church Among Muslims* (Muncie, Ind.: Ron Coody, Union Chapel Ministries, 1988), 87–88.
2. C. M. Amal, "Current Issues Affecting Muslim Women," in Fran Love and Jeleta Eckheart, eds., *Ministry to Muslim Women: Longing to Call Them Sisters* (Pasadena, Calif.: William Carey Library, 2000), 2–3.
3. Nawal El Sadawi, *The Hidden Face of Eve* (London: Zed, 1980), 139–40.
4. Salman Hassan Jabbaar, "The Place of Women In Christianity and Islam," http://www.answering-islam.org/Women/place.html (26 July 2002).
5. M. Rafiqul-Haqq and P. Newton, "The Place of Women in Pure Islam," http://debate.domini.org/newton/womeng.html (26 July 2002).
6. *Ghazali, Dar al-Kotob al-ʿElmeyah, Ihyʾa ʿUloum ed-Din*, Vol. 2, translated and cited in Ibid.
7. Debbie Bartlotti, "Muslim Women in Crisis," in Love and Eckheart, *Ministry to Muslim Women*, 24.
8. Razi, At-Tafsir al-Kabir, on *Qurʾan* 4:34.
9. "Duties of husband and wife" in Mishkat al-Masabih hadith, ET, 1.76, n. 138.
10. "Violence Against Women Highlighted," *Guardian Weekly*, December 1990, 13.
11. Bartlotti, "Muslim Women in Crisis," 21.
12. Maulana Abdul Ghaffar Hasan, "The Rights and Duties of Women in Islam," ed. and trans. by Khola Hasan (unpub. paper presented to the Islamic Ideological Council, Pakistan).
13. Bartlotti, "Muslim Women in Crisis," 23–24.

9

THE CRESCENT AND THE CRADLE

The Mother and Child in Islam

Jill Caner

Few bonds in human existence are as deep and abiding as
those between a mother and her child. It is indeed a sacred
moment when a mother first holds her newborn, beginning
a union between nurturer and child. In this chapter, Jill
Caner introduces the customs, protocols, and prohibitions
of the mother-child relationship found within various sects
of Islam. As a mother herself, Caner offers an empathetic
view into the world of Muslim mothers. Using the shared
experience of bearing life, Christian women can readily find
the means to build bridges into the lives of Muslim women.

THE MAIN ROLE OF MUSLIM MOTHERS

The Ayatollah Khomeini has noted, "If women change, society
changes."[1] What a profound insight into the influence of women within
Islam and other cultures. It is a strong reason why society needs to pay
close attention to the role of mothering. In *Upbringing of Children*,
Moulana Moosa Olgar argues that Muslim mothers play a stronger
role than fathers in educating and training children. Thus, mothers
are the ones who can best educate children in the ways of Islam.[2] No
one would disagree that mothers play an important role in society. A
mother's heart ideally is centered in her family. She should cherish her

children. A common thread runs through Muslim and Christian motherhood, the desire to raise children to adhere to their religion, and to live productive, meaningful lives. Muslim women want to build strong families. They want their children to become ethically moral adults.[3] As Christians, we know true godly nurture can only be found when parents have a saving knowledge of Christ and lead lives of deep commitment.

In a sermon, an *imam* (Islamic pastor) in Vancouver, Canada, addressed the question of how to raise holy children:

> Remember, your children have been entrusted to you by Allah for only a short time, and you will answer to Him for your success or failure to raise them.
>
> Be an example to your children. . . . Remember, your children are watching you. Don't be so materialistic. Spend less money on material things and spend more money on the Islamic upbringing of your children. . . . If material things, fun times, and the successes of this world are all that parents are seen to value, then naturally these are what the children will come to value. So grow up and recognize what these things are temporary diversions which are really not very important.
>
> Fathers, your children's upbringing is as much your responsibility as it is their mother's. Don't become so involved with your career or job that you rarely see your children.
>
> Too many parents come home from demanding jobs and then spend their time "relaxing" in front of the TV. . . . Parents, you don't have time to waste in such "relaxation." Spend your time with your children.
>
> Treat your sons and daughters equally and expect high standards of Islamic behavior from both. . . . Parents, sin and its punishment is the same for both males and females. Expect from your sons the same concern for modesty and chastity as you do from your daughters. . . . Be ready to provide alternative social activities that are Islamically acceptable, even if it is inconvenient for you. After all, they are your children.

We may die at any time, and then we'll have to face Allah on the Day of Judgment. Are you prepared?[4]

A similar sermon on parenting responsibilities could be heard in a Christian church.

The main role of an ideal Muslim mother is to raise children according to the wishes of her husband. With that understood, most Muslim mothers are probably more intent on rearing children who will become good Muslims and ultimately will receive the heavenly reward of *jannah* (paradise) from Allah.[5] Under the theology of Islam, mothers can expect that Allah will reward them for bringing up children who keep the commandments. Muhammed once saw women with their children and said, "These women firstly bear these children within their wombs; then they give birth to them; then they care for them with great love and affection. If their relationship with their husbands is not bad, then those among them who perform regular *Salaat* [prayer] will certainly enter *Jannah*."[6]

For Muslims, hope of salvation is based on works, so no matter how hard they try, there is no assurance of attaining paradise. Therefore, Muslim mothers feel the burden of works not only for themselves but also for their children: "O you who believe! Ward off from yourselves and your families a Fire [Hell] whose fuel is men and stones, over which are [appointed] angels stern [and] severe, who disobey not, [from executing] the Commands they receive from Allah, but do that which they are commanded" (surah 66:6).

Islam's theological system elevates Muslim motherhood to a level of importance higher than that among Christian mothers. It is largely up to Muslim women to rear their children in such a way that they will go to paradise. They see most *akafir* (infidels) as bad mothers who send their children off to day care so they can work away from home for worldly gain or acceptance. Non-Muslim mothers usually are viewed as aloof, unconcerned for the moral and spiritual well-being of their children.[7] In *The Child in Islam*, Norma Tarazi speaks of the different roles of being a father or a mother. She argues that when these roles are not properly played out in the family unit by both parents, the children suffer. She uses Western society as an example:

The conditions of the Western society today can be said to prove the correctness of the Islamic teachings concerning the diverse responsibilities of men and women, of the husband/ father and the wife/mother, within the family. We see what happens if the foundation of security, and trust in the universe as a safe, nurturing place is not laid down in early childhood by the efforts of a committed mother, who is supported and assisted in her role by a caring, committed father.[8]

Christians can certainly agree with Tarazi. There is no greater job for a mother than to be a stay-at-home mom, and it takes both parents to create a secure, loving home. Unfortunately, Tarazi cannot see the more important factor that it takes the love of Christ at the center of the home to foster a nurturing spiritual environment for children. Tarazi not only echoes Christian themes, she actually includes works by Christian family counselors Dr. James Dobson and Dr. Kevin Leman in the bibliography of her book on raising Muslim children. Certainly, it is a step toward a better world when unbelievers seek guidance on child rearing from those who are committed to biblical precepts.

Muslims who live in the United States have the freedom to incorporate Tarazi's wholesome ideals on child rearing. However, in Islamic countries such as Iran, Iraq, and Pakistan, it is not so easy. Males in these countries are at the top of the familial pyramid. Typically, there is a mother and a father in the home—and sometimes more than one mother if the father has more than one wife. Although both parents are present in these Muslim homes, the environment seems anything but wholesome. Something as simple as a family meal does not seem as caring and nurturing as one might think. The males eat first. Then the women are able to eat whatever is left. Even in wealthier homes, boys are given bigger portions and more nutritious foods than are girls. Also, the mother and father will show how the brothers come first in everything, regardless of age. In her book *The Price of Honor*, Jan Goodwin gives examples of male domination in Muslim families. For example, while visiting a Muslim family in Pakistan, Goodwin watched a nine-year-old boy simply glance at his seventeen-year-old sister, causing her to get up out of her chair so that he might sit. The sister sat at his feet. On another occasion, Goodwin heard a seven-year-old tell his mother that she was not allowed to attend a parenting class. The mother acquiesced.[9]

Mothers in Muslim countries have the responsibility to prepare their daughters for the role of wife and mother. Young girls will start to learn around the age of five or six that they should be "docile, obedient, and self-sacrificing."[10] In essence, they will be taught that "a girl should be like water, unresisting. It takes on the shape of the container into which it is poured but has no shape of its own."[11]

FAMILY PLANNING

Muslims take seriously their duty to conceive children. In the Muslim faith, certain times are deemed the best for trying to conceive a child. The best times are Friday nights. The least favorable are the first, middle and last dates of the lunar month. Also, a Muslim woman trying to conceive is instructed to read *doas* (prayers). Likewise, there are certain surahs to read, such as Al-ʿAsr (103) and Al-Ikhlas (112). The couple are to make their desire for children known to Allah.[12]

Conservative Muslims consider *haram* (forbidden) the Western/ European use of birth control. Muslims traditionally believe that their religious duty is to have children as "the key to perpetuating the faith and ensuring the continued viability of the *umma*."[13] Muslims view the Western concept of intentional family planning of only one or two children as heretical. In Egypt, Muslim women have an average of four to five children, not including miscarriages.[14]

Gad al ʿAli Gad al-Haq was the Egyptian mosque's grand sheikh from 1982 to 1996. According to Gad al-Haq, Egyptians had an Islamic duty to produce large families.[15] This ideology is so strongly believed that on one occasion the mosque and the grand sheikh rallied Muslims from all over Egypt to protest the 1994 Population Conference in Cairo. The conference was an attempt by the government to control poverty by reducing the size of families. Western and European organizations traveled to Egypt to present family planning issues and information to Muslims. Through the eyes of the Muslims, however, the conference was seen as a Western ploy to decrease the Muslim population, which procreates at a much faster rate than the Christians. Geneive Abdo wrote, "Sheikh Muhammed al-Ghazali, a leading scholar, accused 'the enemies of Islam of conspiring to bring down Islam and destroy Islamic countries economically and morally.'"[16]

Women in Izbit Abdullah, a village near the Nile River, rely on donkeys as their method of birth control. Gamiya Muhammed said, "My sister told me about the donkey method. When a donkey's breast is filled with milk, I leave the door open and lie on the ground. When the donkey comes and hovers over me, I know I won't have children again."[17]

Muslims look to their prophet Muhammed and other messengers as examples for family planning. Muhammed married and had children. "They are those whom Allah has guided. So, follow their guidance" (Surah al-An'am 6:90).[18] Muhammed encouraged men to marry women who could bear children: "Marry the loving, child-bearing women for I shall have the largest numbers among the prophets on the day of Resurrection" (recorded by Ahmad and ibn Hibban).[19]

THE PRENATAL PERIOD

For married women, few experiences can compare to the excitement, hope, and joyous anticipation felt during pregnancy. Expectant mothers think through all sorts of things: Whom will the child resemble? Will it be a boy or girl? What name is "perfect"?

Muslim moms have the same feelings and thoughts. They also believe they must perform various *amals* (good deeds) to ensure that their child will be healthy and godly. For example, the mother is to repent *(taubat)* to Allah for her prior sins. To ensure protection from adversities, she should perform *salaat* (prayer) in the early hours.[20] She has to make certain she conceals her *aurat* (parts of the body that should not be exposed according to Islamic belief).

Her food should be *halal* (permissible) because this is what nourishes and creates her baby.[21] Muslim women heed Muhammed's words,

"If a woman eats sweet melon, she will give birth to a handsome and pretty child."[22] Muhammed also stressed the importance of eating dates during pregnancy. He believed eating dates would help the woman's body produce a healthy baby.[23] The mother is encouraged to increase reciting the Qur'an and doas (prayers). Al-Fatihah and Ya Sin are surahs that should be read daily. "I seek refuge in the perfect words of Allah from the evil of that which he has created." "The Originator" is one such attribute of Allah to be cited often. The husband places his hand on his wife's belly and recites the words "The Originator" ninety-nine times to protect his wife from having a miscarriage or giving birth prematurely.

Also, there are particular surahs read in hopes the child will be born with a certain personality or characteristics. For example, Surah Yusuf is read in effort to give birth to a beautiful child.[24]

Muslims never escape the yoke of the scales of good and bad deeds. Pregnancy is more than a new and rewarding experience; it is an increase in works. Miriam Adeney writes about the never-ending cycle endured by Muslim women. In Daughters of Islam, Adeney explains why women are viewed as "limited." She tells how Allah, being pure and holy, cannot face the uncleanliness caused by the "bodily processes." Because women menstruate, give birth, suckle infants, and clean up children's messes, it keeps them in a constant state of impurity. In Islam, pregnant and nursing women cannot fast, and menstruating women cannot pray. Because most Muslim women have many children, during their childbearing years they become spiritually deficient, because "every missed prayer and fast adds to a person's spiritual indebtedness. All in all, then, women are 'behind' spiritually. And, 'this [required] abstention from worship is a proof of their deficiency in faith.' Even though they may try to 'make up' days of prayer and days of fasting, they never really catch up with what Allah requires."[25]

BIRTH OF CHILDREN

The long forty weeks' wait is over, and a child is born in an atmosphere of joy. At least the birth of a boy is met with heartfelt joy and pride. The birth of a girl is an occasion for mourning. It is believed (wrongly) that the woman determines the sex of the child, and thus the birth of a daughter is seen as the woman's fault. Some mothers have received a slap in the face from their husbands for giving birth to a girl. Relatives offer words of encouragement: "Next time, you'll give him a son." A Muslim man has the right to take a second wife or divorce his wife if she does not produce a son. For Muslim women, discrimination begins at birth.[26]

Five practices follow the birth of a baby. These practices are not obligatory but are highly recommended. These practices are speaking the *adhan* in the baby's ears, *tahneek, tasmiya, aqiqah*, and *khitan*.[27]

First, the *adhan* (call to prayer) is recited in the child's ear to protect the child from Satan *(Shaitan)*. During the call to prayer, the phrase, *"Alahu ak abar"* is spoken in the right ear. In the *Hadith* it is written, "If one has a baby and makes the *adhan* in its right ear and the *iqamah* in its left ear, Satan will not disturb the child, Allah willing" *(baihaqi)*. This event is performed soon after birth. Either parent or another Muslim who is in a state of purity can perform this ritual.

Second comes the *tahneek*, the practice of placing a small amount of a softened date in the newborn's mouth. After the date is rubbed in the mouth, supplication is made for the child. Any Muslim can perform this. Muslims follow this practice given by Muhammed. "Abu Musa said: 'A son was born to me and I took him to the Prophet, who named him Ibrahim, did *tahneek* for him a date, invoked Allah to bless him to me'" *(Sahih al-Bukhari Hadith 7.376)*. Tarazi believes that only Allah and Muhammed know the spiritual significance of this practice.[28] One can readily see that the practice hearkens to a revision of the story of Mary during the pregnancy of Jesus, as viewed from some six centuries after the birth in Bethlehem.

Third, *tasmiya* is the ritual naming of the child. Muslims are careful to select a good name for their infant sometime during the first seven days after birth. "On the Day of resurrection, you will be called by your names and by your fathers' names, so give yourselves good names" *(Sunan Abu Dawud Hadith 4930)*. It is believed that Muhammed liked names that reflected servitude to Allah. Names that have a bad meaning, are suggestive, or that overly exalt the child are not favored.[29] Also, Muslims do not use names that are identified with other religions.[30]

Fourth, on the seventh day of the child's life, the family is to make a sacrifice for the infant. This is the practice of *aqiqah*. The slaughtered animal, usually a sheep or goat, is a ransom for the newborn. It is believed to protect the child from becoming an unbeliever.[31] It is believed that Muhammed sacrificed a sheep on the seventh day for his grandson Hasan. He then told his daughter Fatima, the infant's mother, to shave his head completely and give silver equaling the weight of the hair to charity. "A boy is ransomed by his *aqiqah*. Sacrifice is made for him on the seventh day, his head is shaved, and he is given a name" (*Sunan Abu Dawud Hadith* 2832). "If anyone has a child born to him and wishes to offer a sacrifice on its behalf, he may offer two sheep resembling each other for a boy and one for a girl" (*Sunan Abu Dawud Hadith* 2836, 2829, 2820).

Also, the newborn's head must be completely shaved. According to the hadith, "The prophet saw a boy with part of his head shaved and part left unshaven. He forbade them to do that saying: Shave it all or leave it all" (*Sunan Abu Dawud Hadith* 4182).

The last of the five practices is *khitan* or circumcision, performed on the seventh day. The Judaic tradition is to circumcise as a symbol of God's covenant with His people. For Muslims, circumcision is an act of *taharah* (purity and cleanliness).[32] It in no way symbolizes a covenantal personal relationship with Allah. In Islam, circumcision is also performed on girls (see pp. 118 and 138–39). For example, in Egypt more than 80 percent of the female population is circumcised.[33]

During the 1994 Population Conference in Cairo, CNN reported on the circumcision of a ten-year-old Egyptian girl. The young girl's wrists and ankles were bound. Gathered around her were her family, including her mother, who was singing. After the circumcision was completed, she asked her father, "Why did you do this to me?"[34] Islamic leaders believe female circumcision is necessary in order to control a woman's sexual appetite. Women are viewed as weak, unstable, and lacking self-control. These leaders are of the opinion that when a woman is circumcised her sexual desires are controlled, which in turn will keep the rate of extramarital affairs down, ultimately preserving the Muslim family.[35]

SUPERSTITIONS

Wherever they live around the world, Muslim families use charms or amulets to ward off evil, to heal, and to bring good luck. Amulets are worn or carried on the body, such as around the neck or ankle. Muslim parents use amulets to protect their children from the "evil eye." The evil eye is "the belief that certain people, if jealous, have the power in their gaze alone to injure or destroy possessions or persons."[36] For example, there are "birth charms" placed on the infant on the seventh day. The charm is made of seven beans and a small bag containing alum, clover seeds, and salt. Sometimes silver or copper coins are attached to it. Some Muslim parents believe they can protect their baby's life from evil spells by placing a penknife on the child. Others will place on the infant a bag containing written charms and a brass disk. The written charms preserve life, and the brass disk protects against the evil eye.[37] Muhammed had his own superstitions. His wife Aishah recalled the following ritual:

> When the Prophet went to bed each night, he would join his hands together and blow upon them, and he would recite over them [the surahs containing] "Qul: Hua Allahu Ahad" and "Qul: A'udhu bi-Rabbi-l-Falaq" and "Qul: A'udhu bi-Rabbi-n-Nas," and then wipe them over whatever parts of his body he was able; he would begin with them on his head, face, and the front of his body, and he would do that three times (Sahih al-Bukhari Hadith 6.536 and 6.636A).

ANALYSIS

How do Christian women reach out to Muslim mothers, who are immersed in the Islamic teachings on family planning and prenatal care, and in teachings concerning the birth of children and the status of the mother within the family? It must be noted that the maternal instincts created by God exist in virtually every mother. The desire to nurture, love, and raise children in a worthy manner transcends culture and is commendable. Few moments in life can be considered as sacred as the moment when a new life is brought into the world. Certainly, Christian women can sympathize and empathize with their Muslim counterparts through these rites of passage.

Given this rich shared experience, Christian mothers can readily find bridges into the lives of Muslim women and earn a hearing for the precious gospel of Jesus Christ. Indeed, the raising of a child from conception through the formative years provides numerous opportunities for friendship and speaking to heartfelt needs. Just as Mary pondered the miracles that swirled around her life and body (Luke 2:19), most expectant mothers are prone to evaluate eternal issues when a new life grows within them.

In an era of lax morality, Muslim women follow explicit instructions to avoid raising rebellious children. Muslims look upon unruly children in Christian homes as clear evidence that we are on the wrong path. "If the Christian God is real," they ask, "why can He not control your child?" In this forum, the parable of the Prodigal Son, the story Jesus that told about a rebellious child who returned to his father, is a tremendous answer. Luke 15:11–32 illustrates the heart of God as Father, in the face of our sinful rebellion. Although Jesus did not apply the story to child rearing, it does depict a common dynamic of family life. Muslim children also rebel, because they have a sinful free will like all humans. As it has in other societies, the erosive influence of modern culture has stirred an epidemic of waywardness among Muslims, as well. What an encouragement that God not only cares for the wayward son but actually stands watch, waiting for him to return.

Islam does not offer any similar encouragement. Instead, it offers only the absolute judgment and punishment of an impersonal being of transcendent purity. The God revealed in the Bible not only judges, but He also corrects and chastises because He cares (see Hebrews 12). He also lovingly awaits the return of His children, and accepts them graciously upon repentance. There is no more fundamental distinction between Islam and Christianity than that the biblical God is Judge and Sovereign—and *Father*— to all who call upon Him in repentance.

Another point of contact is concern about the low worth of females in Islamic society. Though Islam certainly proclaims that Muhammed raised the status of women from that of property and protected them, women are viewed as being in a lower stratum. They are constantly reminded of their lowly status, even at *jummah* prayer, where they have to stand instead of kneel.

Deep within the heart of many Muslim women is a cry for a God who relates to them as worthy image-bearers. The God of the Bible does not relate to women only in relation to their husbands or male children. Yahweh loves women as individuals, *equal* to men in standing before Him. "There is neither Jew nor Greek, there is neither slave nor free, there is neither male nor female; for you are all one in Christ Jesus. And if your are Christ's, then you are Abraham's seed, and heirs according to the promise" (Galatians 3:28 NKJV). In Christ Jesus, men and women stand on level ground before the Cross. Women are inheritors of the covenant and its promises.

Finally, a Muslim woman's constant angst of hoping that her good works outweigh her bad works is exponentially expanded to include the scales that await her children. Can you imagine the deep pain and anxiety she experiences as she watches her children grow, often rebelling against their upbringing? Grace—the manifested, unmerited mercy of God—speaks in a profound sense to this deepest of needs. Muslim women can be pointed to the assurance we have in Christ Jesus—the hope that dwells deeply within us, which gives us hope when the darkest days envelope us.

In my estimation, there is no greater time to reach Muslim women with the gospel of Christ than during pregnancy. They long to know that if they have a daughter, this precious child is as equally precious as a son. They desire to know that God promises that if they raise their children in the admonition of God, then the child who strays can return (Proverbs 22:6). Finally, they need to know that, in Christ, mothers are exalted to a special standing as providers within the home. Notice the reaction of the family to a godly mother in Proverbs 31:10–31:

Who can find a virtuous woman? for her price is far above rubies. The heart of her husband doth safely trust in her, so that he shall have no need of spoil. She will do him good and not evil all the days of her life. She seeketh wool, and flax, and worketh willingly with her hands. She is like the merchants' ships; she bringeth her food from afar. She riseth also while it is yet night, and giveth meat to her household, and a portion to her maidens. She considereth a field, and buyeth it: with the fruit of her hands she planteth a vineyard. She girdeth her loins with strength, and strengtheneth her arms. She perceiveth that her merchandise is good: her candle goeth not out by night. She layeth her hands to the spindle, and her hands hold the distaff. She stretcheth out her hand to the poor; yea, she reacheth forth her hands to the needy. She is not afraid of the snow for her household: for all her household are clothed with scarlet. She maketh herself coverings of tapestry; her clothing is silk and purple. Her husband is known in the gates, when he sitteth among the elders of the land. She maketh fine linen, and selleth it; and delivereth girdles unto the merchant. Strength and honour are her clothing; and she shall rejoice in time to come. She openeth her mouth with wisdom; and in her tongue is the law of kindness. She looketh well to the ways of her household, and eateth not the bread of idleness. Her children arise up, and call her blessed; her husband also, and he praiseth her. Many daughters have done virtuously, but thou excellest them all. Favour is deceitful, and beauty is vain: but a woman that feareth the LORD, she shall be praised. Give her of the fruit of her hands; and let her own works praise her in the gates. (KJV)

Note the following principles from this text:

1. The husband trusts her, he does not treat her as so much chattel (verse 11).
2. Her children call her blessed and give her overflowing respect (verse 28).

3. Her husband lavishes her with praise for her life's work (verse 28).
4. The Lord Himself gives her praise and honor for her reverence (verse 30).

Does this happen in every Christian household? No, but it should. God has called husbands and children to treat mothers with love, dignity, and respect. As Father, God loves mothers deeply.

NOTES

1. Geneive Abdo, *No God But God* (Oxford: Oxford University Press, 2000), 161.
2. Moulana Moosa Olgar, *Upbringing of Children*, trans. by Rafiq Abdur Rahman (Montreal: As-sidq, n.d.); accessible at http://www.as-sidq.org/tarbiyat.htm.
3. Miriam Adeney, *Daughters of Islam* (Downers Grove, Ill.: InterVarsity, 2002), 124.
4. Ibid., 124–25.
5. "The Muslim Mom," http://www.muslimmom.com/parenting/parenting1a2.shtml (9 October 2002).
6. Ibid.,1a3 (25 September 2002).
7. Ibid.
8. Norma Tarazi, *The Child In Islam* (Plainfield, Ind.: American Trust Publications, 1995), 63.
9. Jan Goodwin, *Price of Honor* (New York: Penguin, 1995), 44.
10. Ibid., 45.
11. Ibid.
12. "The Muslim Mom," 1b1 (25 September 2002).
13. Abdo, *No God But God*, 56.
14. Ibid.
15. Ibid.
16. Ibid., 57–58.
17. Ibid., 58.
18. "The Muslim Mom," 1c1 (25 September 2002).

19. Ibid., 1c2.
20. Ibid., 2a1.
21. Ibid.
22. Olgar, *Upbringing of Children*. This work is influential in modern Islamic teaching, cited ubiquitously in sermons and writings on the subject.
23. "The Muslim Mom," 3b1.
24. Ibid.
25. Adeney, *Daughters of Islam*, 116.
26. Goodwin, *Price of Honor*, 43.
27. Tarazi, *The Child In Islam*, 4–5.
28. Ibid.
29. "A Chart of the Manners of Welcoming the New-born Child in Islam," http://www.uh.edu/campus/msa/articles/new/newborn.html.
30. Tarazi, *The Child In Islam*, 6.
31. Ibid.
32. Ibid., 9.
33. James J. Napoli, "Population Conference Gives Boost to Egyptian Tourism," *Washington Report on Middle East Affairs*, November–December 1994, 18, 89.
34. Abdo, *No God But God*, 59.
35. Ibid., 175.
36. "Information About Amulets," http://www.si.umich.edu/CHICO/amulets/amulets.html (26 September 2002).
37. Ibid.

10

WORKING IN VAIN IN
THE IMPOSSIBLE TASK

Teaching the Worker to Weep

Ava Anderson

There is no way to communicate the profound gravity of this chapter. "Ava Anderson" is the pseudonym for a life-career missionary who is serving deep in the heart of an Islamic republic. Her life is always in danger, yet she has committed herself to reaching Muslim women. She writes of the constant struggle toward a "daily crucifixion," and her commitment is a testament to the Great Commission. Thousands of modern-day martyrs-in-waiting are serving in every corner of the globe. This is the heart-wrenching journal, written in narrative form, of one such servant of Jesus Christ.

Arriving for the first time in a northern African country, the young woman realized she had stepped into a new world. Although she had traveled to many countries in Europe, South America, Asia, the Caribbean, Latin America, and North America, this place was like none other she had seen. Its very essence seemed evil. The air was thick with smoke, which in itself would have been bearable were it not for the heaviness in the air. The heaviness came from something else, something unnatural that caught in her throat each time she breathed. The longer she stood there, the heavier her body felt.

Everywhere she looked were men wearing long white robes and turbans. Remembering that she was not to look a man in the eye, she wondered how she would find her friend without making eye contact with a Muslim man. When she walked, no one moved to give her room. In the line for passport control, people pushed and shoved toward the front. Not a single word sounded familiar in the language, and the air was getting heavier. It was not an enjoyable introduction to a foreign land, but no one said this was going to be easy.

As she stood in the airport feeling violated by the piercing stares of men who, culturally and religiously, should not be looking at her, she began to question how she would survive in this culture. She desperately looked for a woman, any woman, to stand next to, to ask a question, to talk with—anything to have the companionship of another woman in this world of men. A few women stood with the men, but they were inaccessible. She couldn't even see eyes behind the veils. As discouragement began to sink in, she spotted the top of a blonde head in the crowd of turbans, *kofias*, and veils and soon made contact with another Western woman.

As the call to prayer sounded from a nearby mosque, she found a taxi driver amid the mass of men. It was Ramadan, and this call allowed Muslims to break the fast that had begun that morning at first light. The grumbling taxi driver was not at all pleased to have two foreign women riding in his car when all he wanted was to sit and enjoy *iftar* (the meal to break the fast). However, he agreed to take the women to their destination, for more than double the usual price. On the way to his car, he grabbed a sack of bread from someone and began sharing it with those walking by as he shoved piece after piece into his already full mouth. Chunks of bread fell from his mouth, but he was unaware. The fast was over, and it was time to eat.

Having completed the day's fast, the men began the feast, smiling and laughing as liquid passed their lips for the first time in hours, and food was once again in their stomachs. Cigarettes added more smoke to the air, making it still thicker and heavier. Would there ever be relief? Why was it so heavy?

Relief came as they left the city. The smoke abated, but the heaviness still enveloped her, sapping her physical, emotional, and spiritual strength. How could she remain and work among these people with such a crippling heaviness? Where were the Muslim women she desperately wanted to meet?

Everything in her life had become a question mark. She could no longer hear the voice of the Lord through the distraction of prayer calls, veils, angry mobs, language struggles, and emotional ups and downs. Worst was the impression of intense sadness and oppression in the eyes of the women; that is, when she could see their eyes. She had been confident of God's calling on her life to serve Him in another land. She had heard the voice of God calling her to go and responded with words similar to Isaiah's in Isaiah 6:8, "Here am I. Send me. Wherever you lead I will go."

Now, she was no longer so sure. At first, the calls to prayer had served as a great reminder to pray for the people she was there to serve. She found it a worthy task to pray five times a day for them as they went to perform their ritual prayers. Yet after a few days, she began to sleep through the morning call to prayer, and the other ones became annoyances. After all, it was not her religious belief to pray five times a day at the sound of a loudspeaker. The people were rude and always seemed to be fighting. In the market a man had thrown glass bottles at her feet as she left a store because she did not buy his precious items. The anger boiled within her, stealing her ability to respond lovingly. There seemed to be little of worth in this society. She had "loved" Muslims before she met them, but now she was tired of the oppression and the difficulty in developing viable relationships.

She had no desire to stay, and a burden for the women of Islam really was not a calling, was it? Everything had been turned upside down, as she realized how distant from the Lord her heart now felt. How could she love God when she could not love His children? How could she love His children when she could not focus on Him? How could she work in a place where there was no joy?

She wanted to smile and laugh, but the Lord had another plan. He was teaching her to weep before Him.

VAIN LABOR IN AN IMPOSSIBLE TASK?

Many answer the call of God by saying, "Here am I, Lord. Send me." Some falter after hearing the call and remain in their home countries. Some devote themselves to prayer, while others promise but fail to carry through in their prayer lives. Some lose interest in their faith altogether and fall away. The obedient women of God are those who answer God's specific call on their lives, whether that call is to remain in their hometown or to go forth to another land He has shown them, in order to work among people who are lost and going to hell without Jesus Christ as their Lord and God.

Islam is an oppressive religion that maintains control by violent means. Yet, it continues to spread rapidly across the world. A quick glance at any map of current trouble spots indicates the violent nature of Islam. Most nations that claim Islam as a majority religion are fighting within their borders or border a warring nation. Many willingly allow radical organizations to operate within their borders. Into such places, God is planting His workers for His glory. Yet, because Islam shows no signs of loosening its grip, many believe the work is in vain. Well-meaning believers often ask those who minister in Islamic contexts why they have undertaken such an "impossible task." Why try to reach people who do not want to be reached?

The answer is that God created human beings to do ordinary tasks, and gave to believers a new heart that desires to do the impossible. Impossible tasks become possible with God, and they bring glory to His name.

William Carey (1761–1834), the founder of the modern missionary movement, once said, "Expect great things from God, attempt great things for God." Is this what Abram was thinking when he set out from the land of Ur to follow God to an unknown place (Genesis 12:1–5)? God told him to go out from his land and his people. God also told Abram that He would bless him. Is it possible to attempt great things for God without expecting great things from Him first? No, because when we work, we expect God to answer. Yet, He does not always answer as we expect.

In the epistle to the Hebrews, the writer mentions several people who lived during the Old Testament period. "All these people were still living by faith when they died. They did not receive the things promised; they only saw them and welcomed them from a distance" (Hebrews 11:13 NIV). Although these people of faith expected great things from God and attempted great things for Him, He did not fulfill all their expectations at a time when they could see it. They continued in faith until their deaths. For centuries, men and women have spent their lives among Muslims without seeing their labors bear great fruit. However, they did not despair or die without hope. They knew that God will keep His promises and will bring all of His children to Him. For the Lord has said in John 10:16, "I have other sheep that are not of this sheep pen. I must bring them also. They too will listen to my voice, and there shall be one flock and one shepherd" (NIV). Similarly, today's workers among Muslims continue in their work, knowing that the Lord will fulfill His promise to bring His sheep into the sheep pen.

What enables these men and women of yesterday and today to continue in their impossible task without losing their faith? Hebrews 11:13–16 gives some insight into workers who persevere:

> And they admitted that they were aliens and strangers on earth. People who say such things show that they are looking for a country of their own. If they had been thinking of the country they had left, they would have had opportunity to return. Instead, they were longing for a better country—a heavenly one. Therefore, God is not ashamed to be called their God, for he has prepared a city for them. (NIV)

Perseverance has always been a matter of the heart, because the workers must be attached to nothing and no one except the Lord Jesus Christ. Yet, they must also be engaged in life and passionately pursuing the completion of the task and the fulfillment of the promises. Workers for Christ cannot do this if they are *detached from* the culture, nor can they if they are *attached to* the culture. At some point, the pilgrim disciple must come to understand what it means to be an alien and an exile in the world. Aliens whose ties are spiritual no longer have an earthly homeland. Instead, they long for the city that the Lord is preparing. The eyes of a dove see straight ahead only, and the eyes of a worker devoted to the Lord have the same unitary focus.

Those who learn this singular devotion to the Lord willingly go "outside the camp, bearing the disgrace he bore. For here we do not have an enduring city, but we are looking for the city that is to come" (Hebrews 13:13–14 NIV). Outside the camp lies suffering, but those who admit that they are aliens and strangers are not ashamed to call upon God to sustain them.

Missionaries who persevere do so because they have chosen to suffer with Christ and seek the city that is to come. No worker survives in an oppressive land who desires to be accepted as a citizen of the world. Missionaries learn to make physical adjustments with a few discomforts. A woman learns to keep her eyes down in the presence of Muslim men and change her style of clothing to cover most, if not all, of her skin. Eating times vary, and the appropriate times for visiting have to be adjusted to fit into the culture.

These simple adjustments do not take into account the greater spiritual struggles and emotional battles to be fought every moment a person lives inside an Islamic society. The heaviness of oppression may cause some to lose their way and stumble, or worse, to become a stumbling block. In no way can Christian women truly become part of the culture, following its beliefs and compromising their devotion to Christ. Being there invites suffering that sanctifies themselves and others.

LOVE IS ESSENTIAL

The more time a believer spends with Muslim women, the more she will begin to understand the Muslim heart. Relationships take time anywhere in the world, but in areas of the world where distrust is a natural response, relationships take far longer to develop. A woman can visit every day and not come often enough to satisfy the cultural hospitality of her host. Or she can visit every day and still know very little about her host's personal feelings and desires.

There is a key to building lasting relationships with Muslim women. God uses people who sincerely love others. The key is holy and loving relationships, not power or witnessing tools. Women who are willing to love in spite of their own and others' faults, who transparently admit that they do not have it "all together," are tools of reconciliation in the lives of Muslim women. Love breaks down barriers, but love comes at a price and with pain. Those who desire to extend life to others cannot always save themselves from trouble, sorrow, and death.

The only way to lift the veil that covers the hearts, as well as the faces, of Muslim women is to love them sacrificially. By entering into their lives, their sorrows, struggles, desires, and tribulations, Christian women can begin to demolish the barriers that have built up for ages. Love is essential every day and all women need to be loved. To do this, Christian women must die to themselves and to their rights. The longer they spend in a Muslim society, the more they will covet personal time. Yet, the Lord was always with people while He walked the earth. Just as He drew away early in the morning to be alone with the Father, so Christian workers will find that early morning is the only peaceful time in the day. This is when their friends will not invite them over or drop by for a visit. Missionaries must redeem this time in order to stay close to the Lord.

Muslim societies are more relational than many other cultures, but relationships are formed over decades, not weeks. Believers must be patient and allow love to guide all relationships. Women know when someone cares for them and when they are being used. They will know we are Christians by our love (see 1 John 4:10–12). As much as believers desire to know Muslim women, the Muslim women need to know the love of God through Christian witnesses.

SOW WITH TEARS

Tears express love in many cultures. Tears show a willingness to be humbled and to long passionately and intently to the point of brokenness. The importance of tears in a Muslim society cannot be underestimated. Iranian women have tear bottles—glass bottles that were once used to catch a woman's tears while her husband was away fighting. When he returned, she would show him her tear bottle, and he would know how much she had longed for him during his absence from her. Here was a visible example of her desire and love for her spouse, and her distress and anguish at his absence. The spouse would see the tears and respond to her in accord with the amount of tears shed. Many women no doubt added some "artificial tears" so the husband would not be disappointed by the amount of her longing for him.

Believers and workers cannot discount the importance of tears to the Lord. One translation of Psalm 56:8 offers the picture of a skin flask or bottle into which tears are collected: "Thou hast taken account of my wanderings; Put my tears in Thy bottle. Are they not in Thy book?" (NASB). An alternative rendering is that the tears are recorded on a skin, as in a scroll. The Lord records our tears. Throughout history, He has seen the tears of His children and has heard their weeping, grief, and pain. The Lord responds to His people as they cry out to Him in words and tears. Exodus 2:23–25 says, "The sons of Israel sighed because of the bondage, and they cried out; and their cry for help because of their bondage rose up to God. So God heard their groaning; and God remembered His covenant with Abraham, Isaac, and Jacob. And God saw the sons of Israel, and God took notice of them" (NASB).

Hannah, the mother of Samuel, was barren for most of her life. She was distressed about this, and each year she would weep and fast before the Lord. According to 1 Samuel 1:10, "She, greatly distressed, prayed to the LORD and wept bitterly" (NASB). She was pouring out her soul before the Lord, and He answered her in due time, giving her a son, Samuel.

The Lord hears the cries and sees the tears of His children and He responds in due time. Could it be that He responds when the tear bottle is full? The Lord knows the perfect time; His children do not. Throughout history the Lord has responded to the brokenness of His children, when they have come to the end of themselves and He is all they have left.

Thus says the LORD, "A voice is heard in Ramah, Lamentation and bitter weeping. Rachel is weeping for her children; She refuses to be comforted for her children, Because they are no more." Thus says the LORD, "Restrain your voice from weeping, And your eyes from tears; For your work shall be rewarded," declares the LORD, "And they shall return from the land of the enemy. And there is hope for your future," declares the LORD, "And your children will return to their own territory. (Jeremiah 31:15–17 NASB)

What about those who are not God's children? What about the women of Islam, who are headed to hell? They have no hope or future, and their lives are like those King Solomon talks about in Ecclesiastes 4:1: "Then I looked again at all the acts of oppression which were being done under the sun. And behold I saw the tears of the oppressed and that they had no one to comfort them; and on the side of their oppressors was power, but they had no one to comfort them" (NASB).

Such are the women of Islam. Their names and faces are unique, but their oppression, especially in conservative societies, is similar. Their lives lack hope, and fear controls their actions. Many fathers and husbands do not allow them to leave the house without permission, and seldom may they be out alone. When they are outside, they must wear clothing that covers their bodies completely, often including hands and feet. When a male visitor comes to the home, they remain covered. Many are required to wear a veil that allows only their eyes to be seen. Others have more freedom, and the veil covers only the head, leaving the face visible. Some wear a veil that covers them completely, so that they cannot see clearly through the cloth and they stumble as they walk.

The oppressors of Islam are powerful and allow little, if any, freedom. Women can be beaten and cursed for wrong actions, looks, or words. Dependent upon their male provider for almost everything, women cannot risk divorce or separation. Many times women abuse each other as they compete for the attention of a shared husband.

Constant worries and anxieties oppress them. A husband might give them a gold bracelet, but without an accompanying kind word or comforting touch. These women shed tears without comfort. They have no hope for a future and barely a hope for the present.

Even their religion is a source of oppression to them. According to their belief system, they cannot participate fully in many of their Islamic religious requirements because they are women and were made inferior. A religion that weighs the deeds of good and evil on a scale to declare judgment is not a religion of comfort. There is never freedom from the guilt and shame of sin—only a need to do more good works so one day the good may outweigh the bad. A woman whose sin is always with her and always pressing on her thoughts is a woman of tears.

These are the women with whom Christian women are trying to share their lives each day. Difficulties arise for these cross-cultural workers, more or less as in other cultures. Working with women in Islamic societies, though, means serving in the midst of oppressed people. The Lord sees the tears of His people and hears their cries. His servants must weep for the oppressed, and He is collecting their tears. The Lord knows when tears are real and when they are false. Whose tears will the Lord record on behalf of the oppressed?

REAP WITH JOY

In dry and weary lands, God has raised up and established His workers. In these lands, irrigation often provides the means for agriculture. As physical waters cause new life in the arid desert lands, so the tears of believers can cause new life in the hearts of the oppressed. Psalm 126:5–6 tells God's children how to sow and reap: "Those who sow in tears shall reap with joyful shouting. He who goes to and fro weeping, carrying his bag of seed, shall indeed come again with a shout of joy, bringing his sheaves with him" (NASB). God's workers who heed His word will learn to weep before the Lord in order to sow His seed. Then, when the seed has been sown with the tears of the workers, new life will spring forth and the harvest will begin. The Lord is awaiting the ones who will weep while sowing.

Learning to weep before the Lord is a matter of the heart. The only way a person is able to weep on behalf of another is to be able to identify with that person. For many female workers in Muslim lands, this means wearing a veil and limiting their movement outside. However, identifying with someone entails more than simply wearing similar clothes and restricting movement. It is about the joining of two hearts to feel the joy, the sadness, and the pain of life. Christian women must understand what it means to Muslim women to miss curfew. They must know their Muslim friends' family roots, family celebrations, and personal desires, passions, and heartaches. These things take time to learn, and the effort is hampered by language differences and cultural norms and innuendos.

Some workers thrive in this environment, whereas others struggle intensely to maintain relationships that bring hope. The work is not easy in any environment, but it is more difficult in an oppressive culture. God heard the cry of His children under the oppression of the Egyptians. He can hear the cry of His people who are crying out for Muslim women around the world.

Is God calling out a weeping generation to comfort those who are oppressed?

The women of Islam will be reached through the love and tears of women who long to see them come to Christ. He will turn their mourning into gladness, and all will rejoice to see these women become sisters in the Lord. The day is near, but the Lord is waiting to bring the harvest. Perhaps there are more tears to be shed before the timing is perfect.

The Lord taught His worker to weep before His throne. She had desired a land of joy in which to work, but He took her and showed her the hearts of her neighbors. How could she desire to leave for a place of joy when there was a land with no light in it? Could she leave her friends who dance and sing every time she visits because they are so happy to have a friend come? The land outside their home is barren and lifeless. Inside, their home is dull and void of life, as well. They have a small garden to water each day to grow a few flowers.

As she gazes upon the new life in the ground, tears begin to fall down her cheeks. The Lord is catching her tears, but when will it be enough to bring the harvest?

The worker expects great things from the Lord. She is dancing in the fields, and the harvest is plentiful. Joy reigns supreme and all are dancing joyously at the work of the Lord. He waited until the tears had been collected. Hearts were broken over the plight of the women, and women were weeping on behalf of other women around the world. The Lord rewards the labor of His children.

Slowly, Muslim women are beginning to come to the Lord, because Christian workers have surrendered to Him in a harsh land.

11

PRAYING FOR ISLAMIC WOMEN

Debora DeVore Brunson

Most Christians assume that cross-cultural evangelism begins with a solid understanding of the beliefs of other cultures, worldviews, and philosophies. Yet Bible believers know that the worldwide missionary endeavor to reach more than one billion Muslims rises or falls on prayer. Nothing of eternal significance has ever come from God without the fervent and prevailing prayer of believers. Few Christians understand this principle better than Debora Brunson. A Christian with a deep devotion and powerful prayer life, she endeavors to give specific instruction how you and your church can begin a concerted effort of prayer for a people who comprise fully one-fifth of the world's population. For more than fifteen years, she has prayed specifically for Muslim women. In this chapter, she invites you to join her in seeking the heart of God.

I pray that the eyes of your heart may be enlightened, so that you may know what is the hope of His calling, what are the riches of the glory of His inheritance in the saints, and what is the surpassing greatness of His power toward us who believe. (Ephesians 1:18 NASB)

Her eyes were mesmerizing. When I first saw the cover of *National Geographic* magazine in June 1985, there was something in the sea green eyes of the young Islamic Afghan women on the cover that caused me to stop and stare. Far more than beauty, there was an emptiness and a sorrow evident that drew me into her heart. The *National Geographic* photographer, Steve McCurry, also noted something in her eyes and mentioned them in the accompanying article: "They are haunted and haunting, and in them you can read the tragedy of a land drained by war."

In June 1985, I began praying earnestly for the women of Islam. As I looked into the eyes of this young woman, it was as if the Lord allowed me to look into her very soul and see the emptiness, the longing, the despair. This young woman represented a world lost without a Savior. Though she was trapped in the Islamic religion, her eyes spoke volumes about the need for a relationship with God. With a new zeal and a passion, I determined to pray for all those in the world who are seeking the Savior, and to pray, in particular, for the women of Islam. Little did I realize that God would one day use my family to minister directly to these precious people.

Where do we begin to pray for the women of Islam? First, we must gain an understanding of their lives. It is mind-boggling to realize that one out of ten people in the world is a Muslim woman. Typically, they can be found in one of five categories: (1) Bedouin women; (2) village women; (3) educated professionals; (4) religious fundamentalists; and (5) political activists. Economically, socially, and politically, the women of Islam fit into various roles in their society. As we pray, it is important to remember that there is no stereotypical model of an Islamic woman.

Second, we need to pray that the Lord will use us to reach these women who are precious to Him. We need to ask that He will place on our hearts the burden to pray for them. Matthew 9:37–38 states: "The harvest truly is plenteous, but the labourers are few. Pray ye therefore the Lord of the harvest, that he will send forth labourers into his harvest" (KJV).

The particular action called for in this passage is prayer. The language Jesus uses here refers to prayer that springs from a sense of need. As co-laborers with Jesus, we should be driven to pray for the women of Islam. Our prayer must be that Jesus will use us in His harvest to reach these women. Only then will our prayer lives take on a new dimension as we seek to be laborers in the eternal harvest.

PRAYER OUT OF REAL PASSION

Jesus' ministry while here on earth was one of reaching out in compassion with a passion for individual needs. Time after time, He looked beyond exterior facades to the very hearts of the people. He saw a hurting humanity, and He saw individuals needing a Savior: "And Jesus, when he came out, saw much people, and was moved with compassion toward them, because they were as sheep not having a shepherd: and he began to teach them many things" (Mark 6:34 KJV). Mark uses a pastoral metaphor to describe the scene. Jesus sees the crowd pressing in on Him as sheep without a shepherd. The writer pictures Jesus, the great Shepherd, helping the weak and helpless sheep. He sees a whole group of people who lack direction and purpose, like sheep without a shepherd. Though Jesus saw the multitude, He also saw individual hurts and needs, and the hopelessness of individual lives.

Hopelessness pervades Islamic culture, but especially the lives of women. We know, as Christians, that it is impossible to do enough good works to get into heaven. Only faith in Christ saves us for eternity. We read in Ephesians 2:8–9: "For by grace are ye saved through faith; and that not of yourselves: it is the gift of God: Not of works, lest any man should boast" (KJV).

Islam teaches that there is no hope for the future unless one is especially good at pleasing Allah. Salvation is earned through good works (surah 3:31). Even then, one is never assured of salvation. Good works can give one the hope of heaven, but there is no guarantee in this life. Only on judgment day will one know for certain if he or she has attained heaven or hell. According to the Qur'an, heaven can be earned by good works if the believer is careful to fulfill the religious obligations ("straight path") and does other duties to make up for shortcomings. The Qur'an states: "Then those whose balance [of good deeds] is heavy, they will attain salvation: but those whose balance is light will be those who have lost their souls; in Hell will they abide" (surah 23:102–3). Islam offers uncertainty, but Christ offers the certainty of heaven, because Jesus Christ paid the price in full on the cross of Calvary for all who would believe.

For Muslim women, the future is one of despair, because they have even less to look forward to in paradise than do the men. They will still be catering to the desires of men. A former missionary to the Muslim world once told me, "When I imagine a typical Muslim woman, I see someone with no hope, resigned to her position in life, no sense of self-worth, and no sense of her value to society. I see subservience, oppression, despair." Without Christ, the situation is hopeless. We must pray with real passion that the eyes of these women will be opened, so that they will see that they can have hope through a relationship with Jesus.

As we pray for the women of Islam, we must realize that Satan has veiled the eyes of unbelievers, and our prayer must be that the veil be removed. It is a spiritual battle to reach Muslims, because the gospel "is hid to them that are lost: In whom the god of this world hath blinded the minds of them which believe not, lest the light of the glorious gospel of Christ, who is the image of God, should shine unto them" (2 Corinthians 4:3–4 KJV).

Those who do not know Christ as Savior are described as "veiled" in their understanding. That spiritual covering is only done away with in Christ. As Christians, we must passionately pray that the Lord will remove the spiritual veil from these women so that the gospel of Jesus can penetrate their hearts. Satan has blinded their spiritual understanding, and as with any unbelieving population, the Holy Spirit must batter strongholds and open fertile hearts to hear the good news of Christ. In Ephesians 6:12, Paul states: "For we wrestle not against flesh and blood, but against principalities, against powers, against the rulers of the darkness of this world, against spiritual wickedness in high places" (KJV).

Any time we seek to evangelize the lost, we engage in combat in the spiritual realm with the enemy, the god of this world, Satan. The battle is very real, but we must realize that God has equipped us with every spiritual weapon we need. Ephesians 6 describes the spiritual armor we must take on in order to be used by God in this spiritual battle. As we enter the front lines of this conflict in praying for the women of Islam, we must remember that the ultimate war has already been won. Therefore, we can pray with boldness and confidence for these precious women, "because greater is he that is in you, than he that is in the world" (1 John 4:4 KJV).

After seven years of investing her life in the lives of Muslim women, missionary Julia Colgate described Muslim evangelism as "an investment of the heart." It is indeed a heart commitment to which we are called, and we must pray with real passion for these women. Prayer is the very heartbeat of our commitment. In an interview three years after her conversion to Christianity, one formerly devout Muslim woman shared specific ways in which we can pray for Muslim women:

1. Muslims believe that the Bible has been changed, and its words are now corrupted. Pray that they will come to believe that God's Word is authentic and stands forever. Pray that their hearts will be open to reading the Bible.

2. Muslims believe that Jesus was never crucified. God sent someone who looked like Him to be crucified in His place. Pray that God will show Muslims the truth about Christ's death and resurrection.

3. Muslims fear God's wrath and strive to earn His favor, and thereby heaven, by doing good deeds. Pray they will see that they already have God's favor; that He loves them so much that He sent His only Son to die for them.

4. Muslim women are oppressed by the religion of Islam. Pray that God will open their eyes to see how Jesus treated women compared to how Muhammed treated them. Pray that they will see how valuable they are to God and how Jesus liberated them.

5. Muslim women are afraid to convert to Christianity for fear of disgracing their families. Pray that God will give them courage to search for His truth and strength to receive it. Pray for God's protection over them.

6. Because Muslim women think that the women they see on American television are Christian women, they believe that Christian women are exploited. Pray that God will remove this misconception, as well as other misconceptions about Christianity.

7. Pray that God will surround Muslim women in Western countries with godly Christian women who will love and reach out to them.

8. Pray that Christian women will not shy away from reaching out to Muslim women out of fear that they lack a complete knowledge of Islam. Pray for Christian women to realize that they only need to understand their own faith to effectively reach Muslim women.

9. Pray that the Holy Spirit will prepare the harvest as He works in the hearts of Muslim women. Pray that the number of Christian workers will increase.

10. Pray that the Christian church at large will have a deep burden to pray for Muslims, particularly those in the countries where Christians are living.

PRAYER AND RENEWED PURPOSE

Our calling, our purpose, as Christians is not to Westernize Muslim women. Our purpose is to share Christ, who Himself grew up in a Middle East culture, but whose sacrifice and offer of salvation transcends cultural boundaries. The temptation in Western evangelism generally has been to want to shape other cultures as much as their faith. Christ has burdened my heart with the reality that these women need a heart change, not a cultural change. For the most part, Muslim women have a great respect for tradition, honor, and family values. However, they have been terribly oppressed by a male-dominated society and a religion that lacks compassion and teaches divine indifference on the part of Allah. We must pray that God will open their eyes to the love and hope offered by Jesus. In their world, Muslim women are surrounded by dominating fathers, controlling brothers, bossy uncles, jealous husbands, and commanding sons. How difficult it is for these women, who are oppressed by men, to understand that God took a male countenance to show His unconditional love, and as a male offered His life on their behalf.

We need to pray with a renewed purpose that Muslim women will see how valuable they are as individuals to God. Because Allah is an impersonal god, a Muslim woman will be amazed to learn that Jesus has done something just for her, because of who she is. The relational aspect is missing in Islam. Islam consists of what humankind can do for Allah. Christianity reveals God as a personal being who shows His glory by establishing loving communion with His people. We need to pray with renewed purpose that God will soften the hearts of down-trodden women around the world so that they might share in this wondrous communion. We also need to pray that these women will become dissatisfied enough about their distant relationship with Allah to seek an intimate, eternal, personal, and loving relationship with Jesus, the one true God.

Christ reached out to minister to women. He interacted with the Samaritan woman at the well, stepping beyond the cultural prejudice against Samaritans and the societal disregard for women, to address her individual thirst—her hurts and her needs—with eternal water that only He could supply (see John 4:7–30). Likewise, He interceded in the hopeless situation of the woman caught in adultery, not because He thought she had been wrongly accused, but because He knew she was a sinner who needed the hope of a Savior (see John 8:1–11). In Mark 5:25–34, Jesus encounters a woman whose unclean bleeding would have repulsed other rabbis. But Christ accepted her touch on His garment, and then He touched her soul with healing, as only a Savior could.

The Bible teaches that God desires a personal relationship with each of us, male or female. In praying with a renewed purpose for the women of Islam, it is imperative that we remember that this desire of God's will be difficult for women of this culture to grasp. They must be introduced to these ideas carefully and slowly because they cannot conceive of the unconditional or eternal love that Jesus offers. We need to pray that the Holy Spirit will break down preconceived barriers to the love of the heavenly Father.

We also need to pray with a renewed purpose that the Lord will remove fear as a controlling aspect these women's lives. Muslim women tend to be dominated at each stage of life by controlling, manipulative threats. While she is a child, a Muslim girl's brothers may actually be encouraged to treat her indifferently or even cruelly. Her father dominates her life and decisions until she marries. She is then subject to her husband and expected to meet his every whim. She fears divorce or his infidelities. She fears the wrath of a domineering mother-in-law, who likely controls her household. She fears for the health and safety of her children. She may fear that if she accepts Jesus as Savior she will disgrace her family and be severely punished.

Though Muslim women have the primary role in the home as caregivers to their families, they have very little freedom to make decisions on their own without input from the males in the family. To make a major decision about faith means going against everything they have been taught about obedience, respect for authority, and family structure. They can only take such a drastic step as they dramatically come to know the love of God revealed through Jesus Christ. His perfect love casts out fear (see 1 John 4:18). Only through a personal relationship with a loving heavenly Father can these women know real peace and acquire the strength to cope with the consequences of faith, free of fear.

Beyond freedom from fear, we must pray that in the midst of their circumstances they will find the joy of the Lord. Joy is a missing ingredient in the life of most Muslim women. Western news organizations have tried to take us inside the Muslim experience, and women have frequently been interviewed for these studies. Seldom are they shown smiling, laughing, or finding joy in their circumstances. Rather, they tend to be solemn, downcast, and sometimes visibly depressed, regardless of the subject on which they are speaking. Islam offers little joy, peace, and contentment to women. They follow the rules, but they never experience the joy that Christian women have found in knowing their heavenly Father. The Bible speaks much about joy:

- Then he said unto them, Go your way, eat the fat, and drink the sweet, and send portions unto them for whom nothing is prepared: for this day is holy unto our Lord: neither be ye sorry; for the joy of the LORD is your strength. (Nehemiah 8:10 KJV)

- Thou wilt shew me the path of life: in thy presence is fulness of joy; at thy right hand there are pleasures for evermore. (Psalm 16:11 KJV)

- For the LORD shall comfort Zion: he will comfort all her waste places; and he will make her wilderness like Eden, and her desert like the garden of the LORD; joy and gladness shall be found therein, thanksgiving, and the voice of melody. (Isaiah 51:3 KJV)

- Therefore the redeemed of the LORD shall return, and come with singing unto Zion; and everlasting joy shall be upon their head: they shall obtain gladness and joy; and sorrow and mourning shall flee away. (Isaiah 51:11 KJV)

- The LORD thy God in the midst of thee is mighty; he will save, he will rejoice over thee with joy; he will rest in his love, he will joy over thee with singing. (Zephaniah 3:17 KJV)

- [Jesus said,] These things have I spoken unto you, that my joy might remain in you, and that your joy might be full. (John 15:11 KJV)

- [Paul said,] But none of these things move me, neither count I my life dear unto myself, so that I might finish my course with joy, and the ministry, which I have received of the Lord Jesus, to testify the gospel of the grace of God. (Acts 20:24 KJV)

- Now the God of hope fill you with all joy and peace in believing, that ye may abound in hope, through the power of the Holy Ghost. (Romans 15:13 KJV)

- But the fruit of the Spirit is love, joy, peace, longsuffering, gentleness, goodness, faith, Meekness, temperance: against such there is no law. (Galatians 5:22–23 KJV)

- For the same cause also do ye joy, and rejoice with me. (Philippians 2:18 KJV)

- For we have great joy. (Philemon 7 KJV)

We must pray that Muslim women will know the joy the Lord— not just emotional or physical joy, but a deep abiding spiritual joy that will allow them to see beyond their circumstances into an eternity with a loving heavenly Father. Only a relationship with the Savior will bring abiding joy and contentment, as these women realize that their future is in His hands.

Pray with a renewed purpose that Muslim women will find the source of all joy in a relationship with Jesus.

PRAYER AND PARTICIPATION

God often places a burden on Christians as He prepares them for a personal call to ministry. When God called me to pray earnestly for the women of Islam, I did not realize that He would one day call my family to participate personally in reaching Muslims for Christ. Eventually our family was asked to minister to missionaries who serve an area of North Africa and the Middle East encompassing twenty-eight Muslim nations. We led a time of worship at a gathering from across the Muslim world. What a joy to share a week with these families who have devoted their lives to reaching the Muslim world with the hope of the gospel. We came home ready to pray with new fervor for missionaries and for the Muslim world. We also felt the urgency to actively participate in the Lord's harvest.

The missionaries with whom we worshiped related ways in which the Holy Spirit is opening doors to new opportunity for ministry and is softening hearts, especially of Muslim women. They shared that God often prepares women in particular through dreams and visions, which are highly valued in the Islamic culture. One missionary shared that Muslim women have a vast potential to influence future generations. If we are able to encourage women at an early age to think about eternal issues, they have enormous potential to affect coming generations.

I came home committed to intercede even more passionately in prayer for Muslim women, and to pray that the Lord would call laborers to the Muslim world. Sharing with others in my own congregation, I realized that God was placing this specific call to prayer on the hearts of other women. Women began meeting to pray specifically for Islamic women. We believe that God is working in the hearts of women and that more will be open to His voice. We are also seeking ways to minister personally to these women, to be directly involved in their lives. We pray that the Lord will call out individuals and families to serve alongside professional evangelists to accomplish this great task of reaching the women of Islam. Some denominations are already actively involved in this work. For example, Southern Baptists are currently working with more than three hundred predominantly Muslim groups in seventy-five countries. These missionaries saw 3,405 baptisms and planted 121 new churches in these groups. My daughter is now serving in the Middle East. The seed that was planted in my heart many years ago to pray for Muslim women is now growing in her heart. We need to pray, knowing that God may call us personally to participate in His plan to reach a lost world.

In January 2002, a team from *National Geographic* magazine searched for and found the girl with the sea green eyes. After seventeen years of being known simply as the "Afghan girl" on the *National Geographic* cover, we now know that her name is Sharbot Gula, and her prematurely aged face still reflects the difficulties and hopelessness she has known. Searching for this lost woman reminds me of a shepherd who had lost one seemingly insignificant sheep:

> For the Son of man is come to save that which was lost. How think ye? If a man have an hundred sheep, and one of them be gone astray, doth he not leave the ninety and nine, and goeth into the mountains, and seeketh that which is gone astray? And if so be that he find it, verily I say unto you, he rejoiceth more of that sheep, than of the ninety and nine which went not astray. Even so it is not the will of your Father which is in heaven, that one of these little ones should perish. (Matthew 18:11–14 KJV)

The good news of the gospel is that Jesus is the great Shepherd who continues to search as long as there is one sheep that needs to be rescued. This parable describes the intense pursuit by the shepherd for the little lost sheep. We are also told of the joy and celebration that ensues after the sheep is found. It is the Father's desire that all would be saved. He has called us alongside in the harvest to reach those lost sheep for our Shepherd. As individual believers, we are called to seek those that are lost—those just like Sharbot Gula, who are lost but do not realize their lost condition.

In order to positively identify Sharbot as the girl photographed in 1984, scientists used the latest technology. A forensic examiner for the Federal Bureau of Investigation was called in to compare facial features. Comparisons were made of the irises in her eyes from earlier and current sets of photos. After long study, a positive identification was made. Our Shepherd needs no such scientific data to identify us, for He knows each of us intimately. He is the Creator of heaven and earth and the designer of each individual life. We are told in Jeremiah 1:5 that He knew us before we were formed in our mother's womb. The Hebrew word that is translated "knew" describes an intimate knowledge.

God intimately knows us and cares for us, as that shepherd cared for the one lost sheep. The Bible also says that He knows us by name (see John 10:3). This is the message that Muslim women are hungry to know. Allah would never leave ninety-nine sheep to go seek the one lost lamb. But our God would, and did. The entire message of the Bible is that, through Jesus, God can remain holy and still accept unholy people. Let us commit anew to join Him in reaching Muslim women with the gospel.

Is the task too great? In our own strength it certainly is impossible. But we are given a great promise in Jeremiah 32:17: "Ah Lord God! behold, thou hast made the heaven and the earth by thy great power and stretched out arm, and there is nothing too hard for thee" (KJV).

Let us commit to pray with a real passion, with a renewed purpose, and with the realization that God may call us to participate in His harvest as we seek to reach the women of Islam for Jesus.

12

LOVE UNVEILED

Witnessing to Muslim Women with a Heart of Love

Virginia Burns

Most devout Christians have been trained to practice evangelism in their communities. Reaching a Muslim neighbor, however, requires a patience and gentleness that is often lost on our culture. In this chapter, Virginia Burns tells why love is the only Christian–Islam conduit for sharing the gospel. Without genuine, unconditional and unrelenting love, we will never get past a cursory presentation. Few writers have the gift of evangelism that Virginia has demonstrated. Few who lead others to knowledge of Christ have the ability to write with such vivid, passionate imagery. Her words will inspire you, and we pray her example will compel you.

Then Jesus went about all the cities and villages, teaching in their synagogues, preaching the gospel of the kingdom, and healing every sickness and every disease among the people. But when He saw the multitudes, He was moved with compassion for them, because they were weary and scattered, like sheep having no shepherd. Then He said to His disciples, "The harvest truly is plentiful, but the laborers are few. Therefore pray the Lord of the harvest to send out laborers into His harvest." (Matthew 9:35–38 NKJV)

Early one morning, I felt myself being torn from my shadowy dreams to the daylight reality of two young children whispering conspiratorially outside the bedroom door. "Let Mom sleep. We can eat candy for breakfast!"

As every parent knows, a child's whispered words at dawn can be louder than a cannon. My body was propelled out of bed and down the hall in a flight of mercy to protect my checkbook from dental bills.

From early morning until late at night, we live in a whirlwind of words. Chaos reigns as words fight to be heard, like small children in need of attention. Words can bless us or curse us, disable us or inspire us, irritate us or make us laugh. Whether written or oral, words are the building blocks of our lives from the cradle to the grave. People may look to position, wealth, or the desire for things to enhance their lives, but in the end, it is words that translate their lives into gain or loss, success or failure.

In a world that abounds with words of hate and profanity, rejection and deception, it is not difficult to become hardened. But there are also beautiful words that bring abundant life. John 1:1–2, 14 says, "In the beginning was the Word, and the Word was with God, and the Word was God. He was in the beginning with God. . . . And the Word became flesh and dwelt among us, and we beheld His glory, the glory as of the only begotten of the Father, full of grace and truth" (NKJV).

Jesus was born to humble parents in a stable, with the animals looking on. His birthplace was illuminated by a star that knelt low in the heavens to pay homage to the living Word. Wise men came from great distances to bow down before Him and present Him with gifts, to celebrate not only His birth but also the glory of His death and resurrection. The boundaries of heaven were split apart, and choirs of angels burst from the skies with songs of praise: "Glory to God in the highest, And on earth peace, good will toward men!" (Luke 2:14 NKJV).

Jesus spent His life calling the lost. He not only healed the lame and the blind, and caused the dead to rise up, but He used the Word of God to teach the way of salvation. The long awaited Messiah had come. Words swirled around His earthly ministry like tongues of flames. Shouts of hallelujah fell at His feet in worship. Whispers questioned His motives. Screams of betrayal and rejection have echoed through history: "Crucify Him, crucify Him!" (Luke 23:21; John 19:6 NKJV).

Jesus, beaten beyond recognition, was taken to the place of the skull, called Golgotha, to be crucified between two thieves. As Jesus hung on the cross, He looked down on the gathered crowd. His mother and some women who had followed Him stood there crying. Other on-lookers scorned Him and mocked Him; some gloated in ecstasy over His pain. We will never know the words shouted at our Savior and Lord that day to rend His spirit, words as sharp and painful as the nails that pierced His hands and feet. The prophet Isaiah said: "He is despised and rejected by men, A Man of sorrows and acquainted with grief. And we hid, as it were, our faces from Him; He was despised, and we did not esteem Him" (Isaiah 53:3 NKJV).

Yet as Jesus looked down on the crowds of people, He was filled with compassion for them. These same people who were laughing at the blood that dripped from His wounds were the very people He was dying to save. Each spoken word strained His already dying body, but each word He spoke brought abundant life to those who were willing to listen. Jesus cried out, "Father, forgive them, for they do not know what they do" (Luke 23:34 NKJV).

The guards who stood by were experienced with death. It was a by-product of their brutal livelihood. For squads of soldiers who pre-sided over a crucifixion, a special warning kept them in their places until the bitter end. If they failed to make sure their charges were dead, they had failed on their watch and could be crucified themselves. They made no mistake, then, in ascertaining that Jesus was really dead be-fore his body was laid to rest in a borrowed tomb. Evil celebrated as darkness and heaviness reigned upon the earth. Those who thought they had silenced the living Word of God rejoiced.

But as the sun arose triumphantly in the sky on the third day, the empty tomb unveiled the greatest love the world has ever known.

PRISONERS OF THE VEILED CULTURE

Not long after the sun rose on September 11, 2001, darkness again tried to claim a victory. But out of the darkest loss and the most horrific defeat, God can use rubble and ashes to once again bring about victory.

Could this momentous tragedy compel men and women of all backgrounds to ask eternal questions and consider everlasting issues? What we use for evil, God can use for good (see Genesis 50:20).

The ethnic background of the terrorists is not the issue. Evil is an equal-opportunity demonic force, limited to no single race. Those who carried out the attacks on the World Trade Center and the Pentagon acted upon the edicts of their religion, but every person—religious or not—needs to be saved by faith in Jesus Christ as Lord. The most profound realization is this: Jesus died on the cross of Calvary so that Usamah bin Ladin could be saved through repentance and faith in Him as the only way.

Our blind eyes have been opened, as we see afresh the faces of the lost. They are no different than those who celebrated the crucifixion of the Savior, not realizing that it was for them that He gave his life. *Burqas* cannot hide the souls beneath, and we can avert our eyes no more. We can no longer stand idly by as generations of women descend into the abyss without Christ and without hope.

This is a holy war of a different sort. We are not called to kill the infidel, for Christ called us to turn the other cheek. We are called to reach into the lives of those who may hate us, to tell them that Christ can liberate them from lives haunted by the image of scales in precarious balance.

Until we stop being casual Christians, Muslim women will never know Jesus. Until we are broken for the lost, Muslim women will continue to die in their sins. Until we grieve as did Jesus for His lost children, we are ignoring the greatest opportunity God has ever afforded us—to share Jesus' love with a world that is listening. Until we can look into our Savior's eyes and realize that He died for Muslim women as well as for us, we will never see the depth of His love.

Although Christians raised in the covenant community may not be able to remember a definite time of turning from sin to Christ, most can identify a time in their lives when they were in a lost state. Remember when you were used and abused by an uncaring world, before Jesus led you to the Cross? Were you any different than those lost in the Muslim religion? Were you any different from those who drove the nails into the hands and feet of our Lord?

The yoke of sin is as deadening and debilitating as any veil worn by Muslim women. Instead of fabric, lost women wear false smiles and temporal attachments. The lost woman, veiled or not, asks: "Can no one wipe away my tears? The pain of who I am sends me reeling and falling on the hard ground of truth. My heart cries out: 'Am I so wretched, so ugly in my sins, that I must stay hidden beneath my facade, unloved forever? Is there no one who cares? I am broken to hopelessness.'"

It is easy to forget how hopeless we were before Jesus freed us from the mantle of our sinful estate. Let us look at Muslim women from a kneeling position before the Cross. Let us weep for their lost condition, just as Jesus wept for us. Let us reach out with the love of the Savior.

THE TORN VEIL

"Then, behold, the veil of the temple was torn in two from top to bottom; and the earth quaked, and the rocks were split" (Matthew 27:51 NKJV). God instructed the children of Israel to hang a veil between the holy place and the most holy place in the tabernacle they constructed for their wanderings through the wilderness of Sinai. The veil separated a Holy God from a sin-laden people.

At the death of Jesus, God Himself ripped this temple veil from top to bottom, exposing the holy of holies. No longer would human beings be cut off from the holiness of God. Christ had suffered their just punishment, and they could share in His holiness. The same God who tore the veil in the temple can use women who share Christ's holiness. We can share in the work of the Holy Spirit to remove the veil that holds the women of Islam captive in their sins. Satan wants us to feel helpless, to believe that there is no way to reach these women. But Jesus enabled our task. He said, "By this all will know that you are My disciples, if you have love for one another" (John 13:35 NKJV).

The congregation of which I am a member sponsors a weeklong children's outreach at a neighborhood park near our building. One year our pastor asked me to talk to the workers from a local day care center, who were transporting children between day care and this vacation Bible school. Six workers sat in the shade of a pavilion, between a noisy playground and the area where more than two hundred children were involved in our activities. The noise level was incredible. It was difficult to be heard, and I began praying that God would give me an opportunity and the words to reach these women for Him.

Among the women was a young Muslim girl from Turkey who was just barely out of her teens. She was beautiful, yet she carried an obvious animosity toward us. My heart ached as I tried to engage her in conversation, but her replies were cold and terse. She had drawn a mental line between us, and she made it obvious that I was not welcome to cross it. Her eyes flashed lightning bolts as the rest of us talked about the material we were using to instruct the children.

She used her voice as a weapon to drown out my words, which wasn't difficult since I have a rather soft voice. Two of the other women were Christians, and I asked if they had any prayer requests, then I asked them if I could pray with them.

As we began praying, the noise of the children and the Muslim women was deafening. I prayed for their needs, and suddenly there was an oasis of quiet, except for the young Muslim woman. I began praying that God would anoint my sisters with boldness to testify of the love of Jesus. It was dead still by this time and I began thanking Jesus for His great love not only for His followers but also for those who did not know Him yet. I thanked Him for dying on the cross in our place for our sins to make a way for us to be in heaven with Him. When I said "Amen" and opened my eyes, the Muslim woman looked at me questioningly, and then dropped her eyes. It was not my words but God's love that had silenced her. No one can stand against the unconditional love of Christ.

"But the fruit of the Spirit is love, joy, peace, longsuffering, kindness, goodness, faithfulness, gentleness, self-control. Against such there is no law" (Galatians 5:22–23 NKJV). It is no mistake that love comes first in this list of spiritual fruit. As Paul says in 1 Corinthians 13:1, "Though I speak with the tongues of men and of angels, but have not love, I have become sounding brass or a clanging cymbal" (NKJV). Without love, even the other fruits of the Spirit can become just loud, confusing noise. Historically, Christians have been hesitant to show the love of Christ to the Muslim nations. The love we demonstrate in Christ's name will quiet the storms of words that have swirled throughout the centuries, belying our mutual distrust and, frequently, our mutual hatred. If we truly want to witness to Muslim women, we have to let love proceed.

PREPARING TO SHARE

Jesus spent three years training his disciples. Paul spent three years studying the life of Jesus and his teachings before he went on his mission trips. We need to temper our missionary zeal with a season of prayer and study in God's Word, and in becoming familiar with the teachings of the Qur'an, so that we are not offensive, nor reduced to defensiveness, when we share God's love. Do not study to build up opposition, but as Paul says, "Avoid foolish disputes, genealogies, contentions, and strivings about the law; for they are unprofitable and useless" (Titus 3:9 NKJV).

Let us strive instead to share the life-changing words of Jesus, "Come to Me, all you who labor and are heavy laden, and I will give you rest. Take My yoke upon you and learn from Me, for I am gentle and lowly in heart, and you will find rest for your souls" (Matthew 11:28–29 NKJV).

Religion argues, but Jesus saves. Reza F. Safa, once a Shiʾite Muslim but now a devout Christian, said, "We are all attracted to Jesus through our different needs. Some people need healing, others need love; all need forgiveness, others need acceptance. God met each need through His Word. The gospel gives us faith in Jesus, and that faith brings us to God. The key to man's salvation is in the gospel: 'So then faith comes by hearing, and hearing by the word of God'" (Romans 10:17 NKJV).[1]

Jesus had great compassion for women. He came to them, in the midst of their daily struggles and self-doubts. Women cast aside by others as inconsequential were lifted up to become daughters of the

King. He changed the woman at the well from a worthless Samaritan into the first woman evangelist. He directed Martha's eyes from the struggles of this life to visions of eternal glory. He purged Mary Magdalene of possession by seven demons and all the resulting emotional damage and counted her worthy to be the first to know of His resurrection. Consequently, she was first to share the gospel. In every case, Jesus met women where they were and drew them to Himself.

Muslim women often feel stripped of dignity and consigned by their culture to second-class status, or worse. They may encounter severe physical and emotional abuse. In their book *Prisoners of Hope*, Dayna Curry and Heather Mercer tell the story of a young girl who was made to feel so worthless that she set herself on fire, preferring death to the pain of abuse.[2]

American-born Christine was vulnerable after the breakup of her first marriage. Confused and hurting, she married a Muslim man and lived with him in Israel. Within a short time, his family began to abuse her verbally, quickly wearing her down to a feeling of worthlessness. She was told that she was just a stupid American and too ignorant to learn anything new, such as how to cook the local cuisine.

As in most abusive situations, she was isolated with her abusers, never allowed out alone and always watched. If she did not answer the phone promptly, she was grilled. One afternoon, as she was out in her yard watering the lawn, the phone rang. She ran into the house to answer it, but whoever it was had already hung up. As she started to walk away, the phone rang again, and it was her husband demanding to know where she had been. When she explained that she had just been outside watering the lawn, he threatened, "That lawn had better be wet when I get home!"

Christine's only friend was her sister-in-law, Marna, who was the mother of thirteen children. Marna was worn out and covered with the scars of many beatings. The two women quickly bonded and were able to share their fears and tears. One day Marna's husband came home with the news that he would add a second story onto their house because he was bringing home a new wife. He expected Marna to live downstairs with all the children, and become a maid to the new wife.

When Marna refused, her husband divorced her, leaving her and their children to fend for themselves.

Christine spent her time in hopelessness, seeing no way out of her situation. After twelve years, her own family helped her escape from this living nightmare.

Be sensitive to the leading of the Holy Spirit when meeting hurting and emotionally injured women. Jesus treated women with respect and love. We need to follow His example of gentleness in Isaiah 42:3, "A bruised reed He will not break" (NKJV).

What type of love builds bridges into the lives of all women? Here are nine suggestions for a gentle Christian witness to Muslim women:

1. *Respectful love.* Approach Muslim women with love and respect, meeting them where they are, at the point of their need. "Love suffers long and is kind" (1 Corinthians 13:4 NKJV).

2. *Prayerful love.* Carry the needs of Muslim women before the Lord daily. "The joy of the LORD is your strength" (Nehemiah 8:10 NKJV).

3. *Safe love.* Let your friendship be a safe haven where hope can grow. "These things I have spoken to you, that in Me you may have peace. In the world you will have tribulation; but be of good cheer, I have overcome the world" (John 16:33 NKJV).

4. *Patient love.* Have the same patience that Christ has shown for you. "I, therefore, the prisoner of the Lord, beseech you to walk worthy of the calling with which you were called, with all lowliness and gentleness, with longsuffering, bearing with one another in love" (Ephesians 4:1–2 NKJV).

5. *Honest love.* Be honest and open in your relationship, directing them to Jesus, that He might receive the increase, for it is by His grace we are saved. "For His merciful kindness is great toward us, and the truth of the LORD endures forever" (Psalm 117:2 NKJV).

6. *Ministering love.* Have the heart of the widow who gave all she had (see Luke 21:1–4). "O my soul, you have said to the LORD, 'You are my Lord, my goodness is nothing apart from You'" (Psalm 16:2 NKJV).

7. *Love centered on Jesus.* Remember how Jesus sweat great drops of

blood, praying for you in the Garden? "Let this mind be in you which was also in Christ Jesus, who, being in the form of God, did not consider it robbery to be equal with God, but made Himself of no reputation, taking the form of a bondservant, and coming in the likeness of men" (Philippians 2:5–7 NKJV).

8. *Servant love.* While the disciples argued over who would be the greatest in heaven, Jesus, the greatest in heaven, humbled Himself and washed their feet. "But the wisdom that is from above is first pure, then peaceable, gentle, willing to yield, full of mercy and good fruits, without partiality and without hypocrisy. Now the fruit of righteousness is sown in peace by those who make peace" (James 3:17–18 NKJV).

9. *Sacrificial love.* Jesus did not hesitate to go to the cross in our place, because he thought we were worth it. "Greater love has no one than this, than to lay down one's life for his friends" (John 15:13 NKJV).

LOVING THE SPIRITUAL ORPHANS

Islam reflects a rich and proud heritage, but it offers no assurance of salvation. Muslim scholars note that if Islam is a religion of works, it must first proceed with a change of heart and faith. Yet even faithful Muslims know that it is a race against time to amass enough good deeds, motivations, and protocols, in order to enter into paradise. Surah 23:102–3 speaks explicitly of the scales that hang in the balance: "Then those whose balance [of good deeds] is heavy, they will be successful. But those whose balance is light, will be those who have lost their souls; in Hell will they abide."

The promises of Allah are temporal and conditional, and he can choose whom he wishes. According to surah 11:114, "Allah forgives whom He pleases, and punishes whom He pleases, for Allah has power over all things." For women, the situation is even more severe. *Sahih al-Bukhari Hadith* 7.30 teaches that "Muhammad said, 'I was shown the Hell-fire and the majority of its dwellers are women.'" Add to that equation that a husband holds a particular sway over a woman's entry into heaven, and you can readily see the anxiety common among Muslim women. "The woman who dies and with whom the husband is satisfied will go to paradise."[3]

Clearly, the crossroads for interacting with Muslim women regarding the gospel is the nature of Jesus Christ Himself. Muslims respect Jesus, but we know that respecting Him as a prophet is not enough. The Jewish Sanhedrin indicted Jesus for His claim to be God. A Christian can bridge the gap into the Muslim mind-set with the truth of the divine person of Christ by understanding the Muslim doctrine of Jesus (*Isa*) as a prophet of honor, and understanding the biblical truth of Jesus as Lord.

In a dialogue with Christians and secularists, Imam Saʾdullah Khan outlined the Muslim doctrine of Jesus:

> It is an essential part of Islamic teaching to revere Jesus *[*Isa]* as an upright, exemplary person, a Prophet [of Allah], as well as to acknowledge the purity and holiness of his beloved mother [Mary] as the most noble among women of all times. Muslims believe that Jesus was miraculously born from a virgin mother and had a . . . gift of being articulate as a child, curing the sick, reviving the dead, and restoring sight to the blind. . . . Since Islam does not in any way accept any human being sharing divinity with Allah, Jesus is regarded worthy of the highest reverence and the greatest respect; but not worthy of worship. Since Allah is Absolute, He is neither the father nor the son of any corporeal or non-corporeal being; Jesus is therefore not considered the physical "Son of God."[4]

We see immediately a central dilemma: Muslims respect Jesus as a man, but they deny Him as God. Khan continues his discussion by pointing out the distinctions between Christianity and Islam:

> Muslims do not believe that Jesus was crucified, but rather that he lived and that Allah elevated him to a higher level of existence. . . . Nor do Muslims believe that another person can

die to atone for the sins of human beings. Atonement for sins comes from sincere repentance of one's wrongdoings, and salvation lies in submission to the commands of Allah and doing righteous deeds.[5]

There it is. The central difference. The key issues that separates Muslims from orthodox Christianity are the atonement and the nature of Jesus Himself, as God or simply as a prophet. When God opens the door for you to witness to your Muslim friends, focus on the issues of mercy and grace. Mercy comes from Christ's sacrificial death on the cross. Grace comes from His free offer of salvation. Humankind can never be "good" enough to erase the weight of our sins. Thus, Christ died to pay a debt that He did not owe, for a people who stood bankrupt and hopeless without Him. Either Jesus is who He said He is in the Bible, or the entire Bible is fraudulent and Christianity is a sham. All of Christianity hinges on the claims of Christ, not as just a prophet, but as divine Prophet, Priest, and King.

When Arab Christian scholar Anis Shorrosh speaks to groups, he often distributes a handout on reaching Muslim friends and neighbors. Here are a few excerpts of his wise instructions:

- *Ask thought-provoking questions.* For example, What does the Qur'an teach about forgiveness?
- *Reason, don't argue.* Argument may win a point but lose a hearing. On some points, you can argue forever without achieving a thing, except closing a mind against you.
- *Persevere.* Muslims have a lot of rethinking to do when they are confronted with the gospel. But rest assured that the Word of God will do its work, in His good time.[6]

THE CONDUIT OF GRACE

Pat and Howard Gleason had no children of their own, so it was easy for them to lavish love on the five children of the Muslim family that moved in next door. The children knew that there was always an open door at the Gleason home and plenty of love to go around. Hesitantly, the Gleasons asked if they could take the children to the children's program at their church, and were surprised when they received permission. The children loved all the activities, and were quick to make friends. It wasn't long before the middle daughter, Sufie, decided to become a Christian.

One day as Pat was fixing dinner, Sufie flew through the front door and fell into Pat's arms crying. Brokenhearted, Sufie sobbed out her story. Her mother's father was visiting them from France and had brought presents for everyone. When he saw the cross necklace that the Gleasons had bought for Sufie when she had become a Christian, he had ripped it from her neck and crushed it under his foot. Her grandfather then said that Sufie was dead to him. He refused to stay in the house with her and left.

Pat cried with Sufie over her loss, then she gently reminded Sufie that her grandfather did not know that Jesus loved him. Pat told her that when she was born again, Jesus had given her a gift that could never be taken away from her. He had given her Himself. Jesus would never leave her nor forsake her. They prayed together, and then Sufie went home with a bright smile on her face. The next Sunday, Sufie's mother started visiting the church to learn more about Jesus.

Howard was an effective support for Pat as she witnessed to this family. Knowing that it was not proper for him to converse with Sufie's mother when her husband was not present, Howard carried Pat in prayer, and helped her to find Scripture verses to share with Sufie's mother.

Limitations on oral communication open up a new avenue when your actions must speak for you. Without words, men and women can testify of Jesus Christ. When a man lives out his life as a demonstration of the sacrificial love of Christ toward his wife and daughters, he becomes a living sermon. This type of humility and devotion to Christ will not go unnoticed in a world dying to know what true love is.

Commission magazine tells a remarkable story of a new believer in West Africa who was tortured but refused to deny his Lord and Savior.

After his release, he said, "While I was being beaten, I thought, 'They did this to Jesus too. Why should I be different? Our blood is fertilizer for the gospel. When the history of Christianity among our people is told, our names will be remembered among those who were faithful.'"[7]

Are we prepared to share in the consequences of leading Muslim women to Christ? Are we willing to stand beside them until the end? Are we willing to go the extra mile and take them into our homes if they find themselves homeless? The apostle Paul answered for all the disciples in Philippians 3:8, "Yet indeed I also count all things loss for the excellence of the knowledge of Christ Jesus my Lord, for whom I have suffered the loss of all things, and count them as rubbish, that I may gain Christ" (NKJV).

Julie bowed her head and voiced a prayer at the women's ministry meeting. She prayed softly, asking God to bless the hands of her sisters as they worked to help their church family. No one there knew about the miracle of her life. Julie's earliest memories are of beatings at the hands of her Muslim stepfather. She was beaten for praying out loud, and for telling others about Jesus. As her stepfather tried to destroy her, the pierced hands of Jesus held her close.

The Holy Spirit will prepare us and give us the opportunity to share God's Word. Let us be found faithful to answer the call to take the hands of our Muslim women friends and neighbors and lead them home.

NOTES

1. Reze F. Safa, *Inside Islam: Exposing and Reaching the World of Islam* (Lake Mary, Fla: Charisma House, 1966), 108.

2. Dayna Curry and Heather Mercer, with Stacy Mattingly, *Prisoners of Hope* (Colorado Springs, Colo.: Waterbrook, 2002), 81. Names of the people in this true story have been changed. In other illustrations used in this chapter, names and some circumstances also have been changed to protect those involved.

3. As cited in Ibn Warraq, *Why I Am Not a Muslim* (Amherst, N.Y.: Prometheus, 1995), 298.

4. *Sa'dullah Khan*, "Crucifying Jesus?" in "Ask the Imam" on beliefnet.com. Http://www.beliefnet.com/story/60/story6002 1.html?frameset=1&storyID=&boardID=9064 (4 October 2002).

5. Ibid.

6. Anis Shorrosh, "Ten Rules for Sharing the Gospel with Your Muslim Neighbors," unpublished document.

7. Mark Kelly, "A Window on the World: The Commission," *Commission*, May 2000, 3.

Appendix

OUTLINE OF THE *QUR'AN*

There are many Qur'anic citations in this volume, and the editors understand the confusion that can result among those who have not studied the Muslim holy books. To help readers follow these references, we have included the following table of contents of the 114 chapters of the *Qur'an* in order of appearance, including traditional titles and their translation.

Each chapter is called a *surah*, which means a "degree" or a "step." Each verse of a surah is called an *ayat*, which means a "sign."

The outline benefits from the prodigious work of Muslim theologian ʿAbdullah Yusuf ʿAli in his work *The Meaning of the Holy Qur'an*. ʿAli (1872-1948) memorized the entire *Qur'an* as a young man, and traveled throughout Europe in his studies. Fluent in many languages, including English, ʿAli returned to his native India and became dean of the Islamic College in Lahore. His work is the most respected English translation of the *Qur'an*, with millions in print, and it continues to be revised and updated. The fact that we have included the Islamic thematic references does not reflect the beliefs of contributors to this volume, who are all evangelical Christians who hold to the lordship of Jesus Christ as Savior, God, and King.

Surahs of the Qur°an

	Arabic Name	English Name	Number of Verses	Theme
1	Al-Fātihah	The Opening Chapter	7	This chapter is recited in all prayers.
2	Al-Baqarah	The Heifer	286	Creation of Man, Moses, and Jesus
3	Al-ʿImrān	Family of ʿImran	200	Islamic history; ʿImran is the "father of Moses"
4	An-Nisā	The Women	176	Two sections deal with women and hypocrites
5	Al-Māʾidah	The Table	120	The "backsliding" of the Jews and Christians
6	Al-Anʿām	The Cattle	165	The weakness of the pagans
7	Al-Aʿrāf	The Heights	206	Learn from the past prophets
8	Al-Anfāl	The Spoils of War	75	Fighting a "good" fight
9	Al-Tawbah	The Repentance	129	Life after war and a new nation
10	Yūnus	Prophet Jonah	109	Illustrations of "straight path" in Jonah
11	Hūd	Prophet Noah	123	Noah, Lot, and Abraham
12	Yūsuf	Prophet Joseph	111	The Islamic tale of Joseph
13	Al-Ra'd	The Thunder	43	Allah's revelation of himself to man
14	Ibrāhīm	Prophet Abraham	52	Islamic life of Abraham
15	Al-Hijr	The Rocky Tract	99	Allah protects the revelation
16	An-Nahl	The Bees	128	All of creation gives Allah glory
17	Bani Isrāʾil	Children of Israel	111	Muhammed's journey (Miʾraj) to Allah
18	Al-Kjahf	The Cave	110	The brevity and mystery of life
19	Maryam	Mary	98	Lives of Zakariya and Mary
20	Tā Hā	O man!	135	The Qurʾan is a gift of mercy; Moses
21	Al-Anbiyā	The Prophets	112	Life leads to the Judgment
22	Al-Hajj	The Pilgrimage	78S	Spiritual implications of the Mecca pilgrimage
23	Al-Muʾminūn	The True Believers	118	The Islamic virtues to follow
24	An-Nāur	The Light	64	Social and sexual issues
25	Al-Furqān	The Criterion	77	The criterion for Judgment
26	Al-Shuʿaraʾ	The Poets	227	Pharaoh, Noah, and other illustrations
27	Al-Naml	The Ants	93	Symbolism concerning Allah's glory

Surahs of the Qur'an

	Arabic Name	English Name	Number of Verses	Theme
28	Al-Qasas	The Narrations	88	Allah's revelation strengthens the weak
29	Al-ʿAnkabūt	The Spider	69	Belief is tested by trials, as in Noah and others
30	Al-Rūm	The Romans	60	Ebb and flow of world powers; Judgment
31	Luqmān	Luqman the Wise	34	Named after a wise man who speaks of truth
32	As-Sajdah	The Prostration	30	The mystery of creation and time
33	Al-Ahzāb	The Confederates	73	Proper relationships; Battle of the Trench
34	Sabāʾ	Sheba	54	Truth is everlasting
35	Al-Fātir	The Originator	45	Allah upholds creation
36	Yā Sīn	Ya Sin	83	Wisdom of the Prophet
37	As-Sāffāt	The Ranks	82	The contrast of the end of the evil and good
38	Sād	Arabic Letter Sād	88	Worldly power is fleeting
39	Az-Zumar	The Crowds	75	All of creation points to Allah
40	Ghafir	The Forgiver	8	Allah forgives faith and good deeds
41	Fussilat	Expounded	54	What are the consequences of Revelation?
42	Ash-Shūrā	The Consultation	53	Contrast of blasphemy and Revelation
43	Az-Zukhruf	The Gold Adornments	89	The difference between truth and glitter
44	Ad-Dukhān	The Smoke	59	Pride and arrogance fall
45	Al-Jāthiyah	The Kneeling Down	37	Everyone will bow at judgment
46	Al-Ahqāf	Winding Sand-tracts	35	All creation has a purpose
47	Muhammad	Prophet Muhammad	38	Hostility to faith should be fought
48	Al-Fath	The Victory	29	Victory comes from courage and faith
49	Al-Hujurāt	The Chambers	18	Manners and mutual respect
50	Qāf	Arabic Letter Qāf	45	Day of Recompense
51	Adh-Dhāriyāt	The Scattering Wind	60	Winds and storms cannot harm the Truth
52	At-Tūr	The Mount	49	All deeds will be weighed by Allah
53	An-Najm	The Star	62	Allah is the Source of the Revelation

Surahs of the Qurʾan

	Arabic Name	English Name	Number of Verses	Theme
54	Al-Qamar	The Moon	55	Men reject the hour of judgment
55	Ar-Rahmān	The Most Gracious	78	Attributes of Allah in his creation
56	Al-Wāqiʿah	The Inevitable	96	At judgment, Allah will sort through men
57	Al-Hadīd	The Iron	29	Allah's power extends to all things
58	Al-Mujādilah	The Pleading Woman	22	Ethics concerning conversation
59	Al-Hashr	The Gathering	24	The expulsion of the Jews from Medina
60	Al-Mumtahanah	Tested	13	Enemies of the faith are not fit for love
61	As-Saff	The Line	14	Lessons from the lives of Moses and Jesus
62	Al-Jumuʿah	Friday	11	Community worship
63	Al-Munāfiqūn	The Hypocrites	11	Beware the wiles of the unbelievers
64	At-Taghābun	The Loss and Gain	18	Allah creates all, even the unbeliever
65	At-Talaq	The Divorce	12	Provision for women in divorce
66	At-Tahrīm	The Prohibition	12	The weaker sex should be protected
67	Al-Mulk	The Dominion	30	Allah rules over all
68	Al-Qalam	The Pen	52	Let the righteous continue to work
69	Al-Hāqqah	The Sure Reality	52	Eschatology
70	Al-Maʿārij	The Ways of Ascent	44	Eschatology
71	Nüh	Prophet Noah	28	Illustrations from the life of Noah
72	Al-Jinn	The Jinn	28	The Spirits who are not angels
73	Al-Muzzammil	The Enfolded One	20	Prayer and Humility
74	Al-Muddaththir	The One Wrapped Up	56	Prayer, Praise and Patience
75	Al-Qiyāmah	The Resurrection	40	When man is taken to Judgment
76	Al-ʾInsan	The Human	31	Contrast of the righteous and evil
77	Al Mursalāt	Those Sent Forth	50	Those who reject Allah
78	An-Nabāʾ	The News	40	Allah's caring nature
79	An-Nāziʿat	The Pluckers	46	The parable of the Pharoah
80	ʿAbasa	He Frowned	42	Muhammed encounters pagans

Surahs of the Qur'an

	Arabic Name	English Name	Number of Verses	Theme
81	At-Takwīr	The Folding Up	29	Personal responsibility at judgment
82	Al-Infitār	The Cleaving Asunder	19	The various judgments
83	Al-Mutaffīin	The Dealers in Fraud	36	Against all acts of fraud
84	Al-Inshiqāq	The Rending Asunder	25	Eschatology
85	Al-Burūj	The Constellations	22	Allah watches over his own
86	At-Tāriq	The Night Star	17	The Soul is most important
87	Al-Aʿlā	The Most High	19	Allah makes man capable of progress
88	Al-Ghāshiyah	The Overwhelming	26	Contrast the good and evil
89	Al-Fajr	The Dawn	30	Contrast man's nature and history
90	Al-Balad	The City	20	Mecca
91	Ash-Shams	The Sun	15	Man awakens to his need for Allah
92	Al-Lail	The Night	21	Contrast of night and day as allegory
93	Al-Duhā	The Morning Light	11	Contrast of night and day as allegory
94	Al-Shirah	The Expanding	8	Hope and comfort
95	At-Tīn	The Fig	8	The fig as a sacred symbol
96	Al ʿAlaq	The Clot	19	Man's hardness blocks him from Allah
97	Al-Qadr	The Honor	8	The Night of Power
98	Al-Bayyinah	The Evidence	8	Proof of Islam
99	Al-Zilzāl	The Earthquake	8	Eschatology
100	Al-ʿAdiyāt	The Runners	11	Spiritual power
101	Al-Qāriʿah	The Great Calamity	11	Eschatology
102	At-Takāthur	The Piling Up	8	Focus on the things most important
103	Al-ʿAsr	Time through the Ages	3	Evil comes to an end
104	Al-Humazah	The Backbiter	9	Condemnation of all scandal
105	Al-Fīl	The Elephant	5	Story of the protection of the Kaʾaba
106	Quraysh	The Tribe of Quraysh	4	Story of those entrusted to protect Kaʾaba
107	Al-Māʿūn	The Assistance	7	True worship
108	Al-Kawthar	The Abundance	3	True spiritual riches
109	Al-Kāfirūn	The Infidels	6	Dealing with unbelievers
110	An-Nasr	The Victory	3	Victory is the crown of service
111	Al-Masad	The Plaited Rope	5	The flames of evil
112	Al-Ikhlās	Oneness	4	The unity of Allah
113	Al-Falaq	Daybreak	5	Seek Allah in darkness
114	An-Nās	People	6	Trust Allah and not man

NOTES

1. ʿAbdullah Yusuf ʿAli, *The Meaning of the Holy Qurʾan* (Brentwood, Md.: Amana, 1992).

CONTRIBUTORS

"AVA ANDERSON" has served as an evangelical missionary in Islamic countries for many years. Her courageous work, often perilous, precludes the use of her real name.

DEBORA DEVORE BRUNSON lives in Dallas, Texas, where her husband is the Senior Pastor of the historic First Baptist Church. The Brunsons have three children, Courtney, Trey, and Wills. Their family is actively involved in missions around the world. Debbie is a frequent speaker at women's conferences in the areas of stress management, family, and missions.

VIRGINIA BURNS is a published author and a former reporter, columnist, and editor, whose works have appeared in a variety of publications. A native of Colorado and a proud mother and grandmother, she has been happily married to her husband, John, for thirty-six years. She has been a Bible study teacher since the age of fifteen, and considers sharing about Jesus through her writing and speaking to be her greatest joy.

JILL CANER is a homemaker in Virginia and a native of North Carolina. A graduate of North Carolina Wesleyan College, she has been in the ministry with her husband, Ergun, for nine years. She has one son, Braxton, and also serves as co-editor of *The International Christian Children's Stories.*

ERGUN CANER is a former Muslim and Professor of Theology and Church History at Liberty University in Lynchburg, Virginia. He has authored and coauthored several books, including *Unveiling Islam* (Kregel 2002), and *More Than a Prophet* (Kregel 2003).

SUZANNE LEA EPPLING is a homemaker, pastor's wife, writer, and event director for Come Together Women Conferences. She and her husband, David, live in south Florida with their two children, Abigail and Andrew. They have recently planted a church, The Lighthouse, in Stuart.

RACHEL L. HARDY and her husband, Jeremy, reside in Dallas, Texas, where Rachel is a professional photographer and graphic artist. She also enjoys writing and has held the positions of editor and staff writer for newspapers at two state universities, as well as at The Criswell College, where she is currently completing a degree in Biblical Studies.

SUSIE HAWKINS lives in Dallas, Texas and has been in ministry with her husband, Dr. O. S. Hawkins, for more than thirty years. She is a frequent speaker at women's conferences and teaches a weekly Bible study to women in the workplace. She also writes for various Christian publications.

EMILY HUNTER MCGOWIN is a student at George W. Truett Theological Seminary, Baylor University, in Waco, Texas. She is the author of several published book reviews and articles for such journals as the *Journal of the Evangelical Theological Society*; *Faith and Mission*; and the *Criswell Theological Review*. Her husband, Ron, serves as an associate pastor at the First Baptist Church in Fairfield.

RUQAYA NASER is a former Muslim attending a Bible college and majoring in Biblical Studies. Her story was featured in *Today's Christian Woman* magazine. She travels around the country, sharing her testimony in conferences and women's meetings.

DIANA OWEN is completing her degree in Biblical Studies at The Criswell College, in pursuit of her call as a missionary to the Jewish people and the Middle Eastern mind-set. She serves in the office of Jewish ministries for the North American Mission Board, SBC.

KATHY L. SIBLEY served as a missionary to Israel for more than thirteen years with her husband, Jim. The Sibleys are the parents of two grown daughters, Betsy and Laura, and reside in Dallas, Texas, where Kathy is assistant to the president of The Criswell College. Aside from being a wife and a mother, Kathy's greatest joy has been serving as a pastor's wife and a speaker and leader in women's ministries.

"MARY KATE SMITH" has served Muslim women in Central Asia, the Middle East and Western Europe as a missionary with the IMB for ten years. She is a homemaker, mother of three preschool boys, and loves Turkish food, Christmas music, quilting, and chocolate. Her work as a missionary to Muslim women precludes the use of her real name.

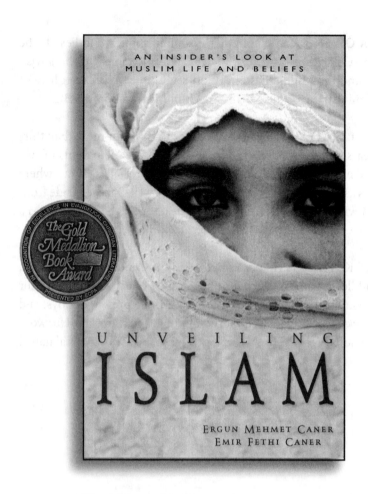

AN INSIDER'S LOOK AT
MUSLIM LIFE AND BELIEFS

UNVEILING
ISLAM

ERGUN MEHMET CANER
EMIR FETHI CANER

UNVEILING ISLAM
An Insider's Look at Muslim Life and Beliefs
Ergun Mehmet Caner & Emir Fethi Caner
0-8254-2400-3

Discover the reality of Islam—written by two former Sunni Muslims widely respected for their ability to clearly explain the Muslim mind. Also available in Spanish.

"Must reading for all Christians."
—Zig Ziglar

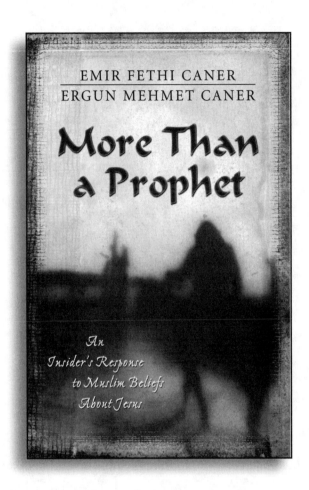

MORE THAN A PROPHET
An Insider's Response to Muslim Beliefs About Jesus
Emir Fethi Caner & Ergun Mehmet Caner
0-8254-2401-1

In a question-and-answer format, this book helps Christians reach out to their Muslim neighbors by responding to the most common questions Muslims have about Christianity.